THE CONFIDENT COACH'S GUIDE
TO TEACHING LACROSSE

THE CONFIDENT COACH'S GUIDE TO TEACHING LACROSSE

FROM BASIC FUNDAMENTALS TO ADVANCED PLAYER SKILLS AND TEAM STRATEGIES

By Daniel Morris

Edited by Michael Morris

THE LYONS PRESS
Guilford, Connecticut
An imprint of The Globe Pequot Press

The Lyons Press is an imprint of The Globe Pequot Press.

10 9 8 7 6 5 4 3 2 1

Printed in the United States of America

Practice and play diagram illustrations by Mariel Morris

Library of Congress Cataloging-in-Publication Data

Morris, Daniel, 1975–
    The confident coach's guide to teaching lacrosse / by Daniel Morris ;
    edited by Michael Morris.
        p. cm.
    Includes bibliographical references and index.
    ISBN 1-59228-588-0 (alk. paper)
    1. Lacrosse for children—Coaching. I. Morris, Michael, 1947 Aug. 6–
        II. Title.
    GV989.17.M67 2005
    797.347'07'7—dc22
                                                          2005018948

CONTENTS

ACKNOWLEDGMENTS

I would like to thank the following people who helped in the creation of this book:

Graphic artist and photographer Ron Dubé, for donating his time and the patience he showed working with our young player models, Sean Wagner, Tim Fazzinga, and Kevin Doherty. Photographer Dave Adams, whose live-action game photos bring a level of excitement to these pages. The Lyons Press, for all their behind-the-scenes work, including efforts by Jennifer Taber, Christine Duffy, Jay Cassell, and Tom McCarthy.

I owe a special debt of gratitude to my family for their unwavering support throughout this long and frequently challenging project. First, my sister Mariel, who stepped in at the eleventh hour to create the illustrations that made abstract plays and concepts easily understandable. My sister Margeaux, whose unflinching opinion helps to sharpen my focus whenever I lose sight of my goals. My mother Karen, who has always believed that I can accomplish even more than I imagine. And especially Marybeth Susarchick, my fiancée as this was written and soon to be my bride, whose encouragement and support keeps me moving in the right direction. Lastly, I wish to thank my father and editor, Michael Morris, whose spark of an idea became the book you are holding. I truly could not have done this without his experience, guidance and determination.

This book is dedicated to the lacrosse community – a unique fraternity of players, coaches, and fans who continue to make this the fastest-growing, greatest game in sports.

Daniel M. Morris
October 20, 2005

INTRODUCTION

You've just been handed a challenging new assignment—teaching and coaching lacrosse to a group of youngsters who may know little or nothing about the game.

Where do you begin? And how do you make their introduction to this sport fun, engaging, and exciting, all while you impart the fundamental skills they will need to play well and, hopefully, excel when they take the field?

Another concern arises for coaches who themselves have scant knowledge or experience with lacrosse. Although it is one of the fastest-growing team sports in this country, lacrosse has nowhere near the following of other essential, "all-American" sports such as baseball, basketball, and football, and in terms of popularity in organized school sports it even falls behind that international favorite, soccer. As a result, and despite its many devoted players and fans, the fundamentals, rules, and nuances of modern lacrosse are simply not as well known or as well understood.

This is an odd lapse because lacrosse is the oldest and most enduring game played in America, a piece of history itself. Lacrosse originated among the native tribes of North America and was an important part of their culture long before the European settlers arrived. At that time it was less of a sport and more a test of manhood for the young men of the tribes—as well as a surrogate, often little-disguised preparation for outright warfare between competing tribes. Games were played for days on end, sometimes from village to village on "fields" miles long, using a primitive ball of stitched hides or even a skull or rock in place of a ball.

Advances to equipment and adjustments to the rules have allowed lacrosse to evolve over the centuries into the modern game played today.

For a while it was an Olympic exhibition sport, and it is popular in nations such as England, Australia, Japan, and Canada. Some of our greatest amateur and professional athletes in other sports were also lacrosse players, most notably football legend Jim Brown, who helped develop many of the playing techniques used today and who set national scoring records as a collegiate superstar.

However, even for those who have watched it and are familiar with the game or its history, lacrosse can be a difficult sport to fully understand—and daunting for unschooled players to learn. By comparison, the fundamental playing skills of basketball, football, and soccer are relatively easy to grasp. Manipulating a ball with hands or feet are movements that come naturally to just about everyone. Baseball has the added challenge of using an implement (the bat) to strike the ball, but only lacrosse requires mastery of a stick for catching and throwing.

It is the stick, or *crosse*, that makes this game a challenge unlike any other. But the sense of accomplishment that comes in meeting this challenge is especially rewarding, as so many new, young players are discovering every day. If your job is to teach them and coach them, this book can be an invaluable resource for you and for anyone who wants to learn and play this exciting game.

CHAPTER 1

TEACHING YOUTH LACROSSE

Organized practice in any team sport isn't just a workout, and isn't just playtime. It must have specific objectives. Your players are there to learn *how* to play. Your job is to teach them. This requires discipline, planning, and team-building skills on your part, along with discipline and commitment on theirs.

But that doesn't mean practice can't be fun. Young people enjoy sports for many reasons—they get to learn and hopefully excel in new games, they get to suit up in cool uniforms and exotic equipment, they get to take the field with their pals and test themselves in competition with one another, and they get to play. A good teacher keeps all of this in perspective. When your team gathers around to hear what "Coach" has to say, remember that you're giving them more than just the rules of a game.

The purpose of this book is to help coaches teach lacrosse fundamentals to youths mainly of middle school and high school ages, the primary entry-level group in this sport today. Although much of what is described here may be applied to younger players, despite the growing appeal of this sport there are very few community or school efforts to create "peewee" lacrosse leagues, and manufacturers are just beginning to develop downsized equipment suitable for children's age groups and sizes.

College-level players and coaches can benefit from this book as well, but players at this age typically have more experience with team sports—along with considerably greater maturity, competitiveness, and muscle

Most organized lacrosse today is played by older youths, with school instruction and leagues beginning at the high school level. But in some areas of the country with advanced lacrosse programs, the sport is moving progressively downward into elementary grades and becoming available to junior players. These young contenders play for a town recreation league in Somers, NY. *Photo courtesy of Ron Dubé Design*

mass, all of which have an impact on the approach a coach would take to practice and drills—and they may find some of the information herein to be too elementary or remedial. Finally, this book does not address women's lacrosse, which is so different in its rules and strategies that it is an entirely separate sport. Of course, girls who choose to compete with the boys in men's lacrosse (and today some do) will benefit equally from this book.

Photo courtesy of Dave Adams Photos

Age and Performance

When working with preteen and teenage youths, it is important to keep not only their age in mind, but also the level of performance you can expect from them based on their age. One of the most fundamental problems a coach has to deal with is how to ensure that all players on the team get sufficient playing time in competition, regardless of skill level.

No one wants to join a team to sit on the bench. As a coach, you're almost guaranteed to lose a player or two because they feel they're not getting the playing time they need to make the long hours and grueling practices worthwhile. Other players may see themselves as first-string caliber—whether you agree or not—and anything less won't be acceptable. Instead of working harder to secure a starting spot, or taking a support role, these players often quit. What is most unfortunate about situations like this is that many of these youths don't only leave the team, but they leave the sport forever, and that is a true loss.

Of course, some players will never be happy spending any time on the bench, while others may find they're just not cut out for team sports. That decision is theirs alone, but it is every youth coach's responsibility to get all of his players into games regularly.

This advice specifically refers to "youth coaches." Coaches in competitive high school and college leagues aren't going to empty their benches every game just so all players can walk off the field feeling they contributed. They, and their teams, are playing to win. If these coaches can get their freshmen or sophomore recruits into the action they will, but this isn't their priority. Youth coaches are blessed by the fact that they aren't playing for a state or college championship. They are coaching for the love of the sport and teaching the next generation of players what it means to be part of a team.

Organizations like the Positive Coaching Alliance (PCA) advocate rules that guarantee all players a significant amount of playing time in every game. Unfortunately, there are coaches at every level who won't play less-skilled players for fear of losing the contest. While there is always a chance that weaker players might contribute to a loss, it is also true that even the best players don't always triumph. Whether your team loses or wins, the benefit of having all your players involved on the field, and having each player go home and tell his parents how he played, outweighs a loss any day.

Get Them in the Game

There are techniques coaches can employ to make sure all players contribute on the playing field. The most obvious is to make frequent substitutions when your team is ahead by a sizable score. This is perfect for weaker players because they won't feel the pressure of having to win or have to worry about losing the game for their teammates. If they allow a goal or two it won't be a big deal, and the experience they get learning from their mistakes will be worth it. Injuries and break periods are also opportunities to substitute players. No player should be on the field throughout sixty minutes of game time. All players need a chance to rest their legs, get some water, and even collect their emotions if they're having a tough outing.

A good way to keep weaker players involved is to schedule playing time for them. You can do this by putting them in the starting lineup when you're not up against powerhouse teams, or by giving less-skilled players a designated starting or rotation spot as a reward for extra effort at practices. Another way is to guarantee field time to groups of players during every game. For example, have your weakest attackmen always play the last two minutes of the first half and first two minutes of the second half.

One strategy to avoid is using your least-capable players as a "defensive midfield line." There are two reasons for this. First, your weakest players aren't going to be the aggressive ball-stoppers or defense specialists you'll need in tight game situations. Second, it sends the wrong message about playing defense in general—it says that defense is where weaker players end up, or that players who aren't offensive scorers have a less important role on the team.

Coaches need to encourage all players to take pride in their respective positions, as they all contribute to the team effort. At the same time, individual players need to work hard to distinguish themselves, to strive for their "personal best." Players should not be relegated to positions where they can do the least damage. It's the coach's task to discuss those players' goals in the sport and to evaluate them, playing to their strengths and finding the positions that fit their abilities.

Dealing with Superstars

At the other end of the spectrum are players whose abilities far exceed those of their teammates and who score easily against weaker players. As a coach, you don't want to stunt a star player's development, but at the same time you don't want anyone to grow into the habit of controlling the ball or playing unassisted all the time.

At the youth lacrosse level, when players of similar ages and grades can differ greatly in size, speed, strength, and determination, it can be common for some to easily overpower the others, barreling through defenders, double-teams, and anything else thrown their way. While a coach who is excited about victory might wish to overlook this, ultimately it is bad for the team, and it can hinder a gifted player's development in the long run.

Bad habits learned early are not only harder to break later on, but a coach who fails to rein in a superstar and insist on teaching him to play with lacrosse fundamentals is actually cheating the player out of a proper education in the sport. As others develop, the star player will no longer be able to dominate and may not possess the range of skills necessary to excel against more competitive players. Every experienced coach has a story to tell about a standout freshman "phenom" who burned out early because he couldn't, or wouldn't, adapt.

Drills that emphasize teamwork and ball movement help to defuse the superstar mentality among athletes by demonstrating how play-making and smart offensive and defensive strategies are superior to any one player. Especially with younger players, coaches need to focus on fundamental skills, field communication, and team play to build a solid foundation for lacrosse that keeps players excited—and keeps them in the game.

Managing Expectations

Young, inexperienced players typically enter sports with heightened initial enthusiasm—and often, unrealistic expectations—so there is a concern that a season full of losses will hurt morale and lead to players quitting. What can a coach do to keep them engaged?

Teaching players in their formative years to strive for realistic, achievable personal and team goals is a far more effective strategy than trying to teach them simply to win. And a coach who imparts these lessons can achieve a successful season regardless of the numbers posted in the wins-and-losses column.

The development and implementation of team goals begins with the coach. Passive coaches who don't set manageable expectations, fail to delegate responsibilities to their players, and refrain from decision-making in general typically end up with teams that lack focus and direction. This leads to uninspired players who can't interact effectively, who lose matches to better-organized teams, and who often end up quitting in frustration. Just the opposite is the over-aggressive coach who runs his program like a dictatorship, barking orders and making every decision without consulting his team captains, players, assistant coaches, or anyone else. In this situation, the players are little more than chess pieces controlled by their coach, unable to offer any input, and who are also likely to quit in frustration because the coach has no interest in listening to what they have to contribute.

A good coach doesn't go to such extremes and instead works with his players to develop team interaction along with their personal abilities. This coach can be a strong leader, an authority figure the team respects, but one who listens to his players and allows them to share in the management of the team. A shared sense of commitment among the players promotes both personal responsibility and team pride.

Identifying Goals

Attainable yet challenging goals are those that build success in stages and can be measured at regular intervals. Also, keeping a team focused on short-term benchmarks will help to motivate players from one game to the next, and prevent them from dwelling on season standings and losses. Making an undefeated season your team's goal is not only unrealistic, it also guarantees discouragement among the players with their first unanticipated loss.

Examples of attainable, short-term goals might include striving for 75 percent of the team's scoring shots to be assisted in each game, or shutting out an opposing team for a full period. Once such accomplishments are met, a team can use them as springboards to more ambitious goals. Similar benchmarks should be worked into practices to give the team positive reinforcement on a regular basis.

The same can be done with individual players. A timid player may set a personal goal of taking at least ten shots at the cage during scrimmages, or slower players may attempt to finish among the top half of the team during wind sprints.

Once a team's goals are identified and mapped out for the season, the coach should assign responsibilities to each player and explain how their roles contribute to the collective effort. A midfielder may become the team's face-off specialist, or an attackman with exceptional passing skills may be assigned to a point position to feed stronger shooters. At the same time, the coach needs to identify his players' individual strengths and weaknesses, discuss personal goals with each of them, and develop a training schedule that enables them to work toward objectives that benefit them and the team as a whole.

During each season only one team can win the championship. And for every win a team notches, another team suffers a loss. This is the nature of sports, and the part that builds true character. The most memorable coaches, the ones who make a real difference in the development of young men and women, are those who can teach their players that being a part of a team, even a losing team, can be a fun and rewarding experience.

Coach/Parent Relations

A major concern in youth sports today is interference and irate behavior by overzealous parents. Verbal and even physical threats toward coaches, referees, and other spectators are not uncommon, and a coach must be prepared to deal with unsportsmanlike behavior off the field as well as on. You may find that your responsibility includes not only instructing young players and helping them achieve their potential in sports, but also educating their parents about the value of team sports in their children's development.

By inviting parents and players to meet with you before the season begins, you can establish ground rules for game and practice behavior— on field and off—and prevent confrontations before they occur. Your discussion should include the meaning of good sportsmanship, actions that will not be tolerated, and penalties for inappropriate behavior. Work with the parents to establish ways to control emotional outbursts, verbal abuse, and coaching from the stands. Penalties can include ejection from the field or spectator area, suspension from future games,

Photo courtesy of Ron Dubé Design

expulsion from the league for parent and/or child, and ultimately legal action for incidents that escalate into physical violence. Some youth sports organizations now require parents to sign an agreement, prior to the start of the season, stating they will abide by such rules.

No coach wants to have to deal with volatile parents or spectators. Fortunately, there are organizations geared toward youth sportsmanship and resources to help you manage troublesome issues. Two examples are the Institute of International Sport (www.internationalsport.com) and the National Alliance for Youth Sports (www.nays.org).

You can also use a preseason parent/player meeting as an opportunity to introduce yourself, summarize your coaching philosophy, explain the goals you will set for the players and team, and outline the options parents have in supporting their child's decision to play lacrosse, from emotional and financial support to ways they can positively contribute to the program. This is also a good time to make certain the parents understand that, when all is said and done, the primary reason for playing youth lacrosse is to have fun.

Coach/Player Relations

As a youth coach, your mission is to build a team and create a program that can be enjoyed by all who participate. But young people are easily distracted, and keeping all of your charges engaged and fully involved during lengthy practice sessions is a challenge in itself. Before practices, decide what you want to achieve in the time allotted. Create a schedule that avoids downtime and groups of players waiting around for the next activity to begin. Ensure that sessions move along at a steady clip to prevent boredom and mischief.

Players also need to understand why they are participating in each drill and what they should be taking away from it. For example, if a drill is designed to accentuate shooting while running, make sure they know that this is the point. Otherwise, they may simply try to score and plant their feet to take the safe shot, believing they have accomplished the drill when they hit the net but defeating the purpose of the exercise.

Keep in mind that, especially with younger players, "noviceness equals nervousness." Expect wild throws, dropped passes, and lots of blown plays. Find creative ways to push your players toward improvement. Make sure they are "looking" the ball into the stick. Keep them moving when catching and throwing. Don't assume that anyone new to this game knows enough to know what to do—remember that it's your job to instruct them. Get them to understand that all types of unanticipated situations can occur on field, but how they react is within their control.

To make drills fun, add a level of competition that keeps your players fired up. Split them into squads and pit them against one another. Award the winning "team" a water break while the losing team does push-ups—no harsh punishments, but enough of a risk/reward to make players work a bit harder. Spotlight fundamentals in all drills and stress "repetition to achieve perfection."

Finally, work to build a sense of team spirit among your players by doing things together, both on and off the field. During warm-ups, everyone should be warming up, not just the rest of the team while the star attackman fiddles with his stick. Barring injuries, no one should receive special treatment. From the beginning, reinforce the concept that players are not playing for themselves or for individual statistics, but as members of a team for the success of the program.

A good way to build team spirit is to occasionally take a break from your regular program and do things other than practice lacrosse. Hold team dinners, captains' practices, fund-raisers. Attend local high school, college, or professional games together. Hand out awards voted on by the players themselves for categories like Offensive and Defensive MVP, or an award simply for the player who is most instrumental in the day-to-day running of the program. Create team traditions that foster a sense that each of your players is part of a lasting legacy.

CHAPTER 2

ORGANIZING PRACTICES

Putting together team practices is a continually evolving process that depends on many elements, such as the age group you are coaching, the facilities available (which can change from one session to the next), and the number of players on hand (also liable to fluctuate). Other factors influencing how practices run include at what point in the season you find yourself, and whether your practice has a particular objective—such as preparing for a specific opponent, or addressing a recognized weakness in your team.

As coach, you need to create a schedule and expect your players to show up ready to drill, but you also have to be flexible and introduce changes as required. You may elect to spend more time working on plays or concepts your players are struggling with, or you may be forced to throw out your carefully prepared practice plan because half your team is out with the flu. Although certain components of practice sessions should be dependably unchanging—warm-ups before drills, repeating fundamentals, building team esprit—ultimately, you as coach have to evaluate what type of workout is best for your players at the given time using the resources you have on hand.

Be Flexible

Youth coaches must tailor their programs to suit the age and skill level of their players. With novice players, and particularly younger novice players, you'll need to go slower, you may need to repeat more, and you'll have to keep things moving to not lose their attention. Make practices fun with shorter, less intensive drills. Don't emphasize contact drills as much with adolescent and early-teen players, and start them off with simple, straightforward offensive/defensive concepts and plays.

Older teens and "veteran" players generally need less introduction to practice workouts, and you can expect most to have some type of sports foundation, however limited. With this group, coaches may spend more time fine-tuning players' skills and working on athletic training. Teamwork and team building begin to take precedence over individual needs, more advanced playing concepts may be introduced, and the level of contact and competitiveness increases.

Keep in mind that even experienced players can find it difficult to grasp certain concepts, and younger players are certainly going to struggle at times. Don't make your practice routine inflexible. If you allocated fifteen minutes to work on rides and clears and the team just isn't getting it, don't abandon what you were doing because the schedule tells you to. Work on the drill until you see some measure of success, cutting back on something else that was originally planned.

DRILL POINTS

- Begin with the most basic drills and build from there. Don't introduce advanced concepts until your players have mastered the fundamentals.

- Constantly rotate and change the drills you use so teams don't grow bored and complacent. Mix it up as you go. Keep drills under twenty minutes.

- Use drills in place of conditioning whenever possible. With the right mix of drills, players can get all the exercise they need while they improve their game.

- Drills require discipline, but find ways to make them fun. Create competitions. Reward hard work. Praise your players when they put in extra effort.

Also, take your cues from games and prior practices as to what your players need to work on. Use drills to address and fix problems. If you play a game and the team's percentage of ground balls recovered was abysmal, add more ground ball drills to the next practice.

Running a Practice

Preparation is the key to successful practices. A good coach has his practice organized and ready to go *before* he arrives at the field. It takes only a few minutes to write up a practice plan for each session. Include a number of contingency plans in case the weather turns foul or fewer players show up than expected.

Unless equipment duties are outsourced to players or parents, the coach should show up with everything needed to run the practice. In order of necessity, this includes but is not limited to:

- Balls (five dozen)
- Whistle
- Coach's lacrosse stick
- Clock/stopwatch
- Reversible pinnies (practice jerseys) or two sets of two colors
- Small cones (one to two dozen)
- Clipboard with paper or dry erase board for diagramming drills/plays
- Athletic tape
- Helmet and stick repair kits
- Tape measure

At the start of practice, cages (goals) should be on the field and ready, with nets tightly strung and holes patched. This responsibility can be delegated to the captains or players. Some teams entrust the rookies with the field tasks, some teams have a rotation that includes all players, and some teams may be lucky enough to have team managers. On younger teams, parents may opt to help out, and in most cases their participation would be welcome. You have to make sure those responsible know their role so the job gets done.

A Note about Balls

The more lacrosse balls a team has to practice with, the less time you'll waste having players search for them. Beginning players miss the cage and overthrow teammates on a regular basis, sending balls flying everywhere. Nothing slows down practice more than stopping everything to search for balls.

Make sure your team has plenty of balls on hand. That way, if some are lost or scattered around the edges of the field, you won't lose practice momentum. Line up the team and sweep the area at the end of each practice to gather all the loose balls and replenish your supply.

Making Practice Time Count

In sports, fun and discipline go hand in hand. Instruct players to arrive at the field with enough time to suit up, get taped (if necessary), and adjust their sticks before practice officially begins. A 10:00 a.m. start will soon turn into 10:20 if you aren't strict about this rule, but when you have only a limited amount of field time with your players, every minute counts. Teach your players to show up early and be ready to line up on field at the designated time. Players will learn to enjoy the extra time before the first whistle blows.

Because practices are tightly structured, pre-practice is also a good time for players to come to you with questions, in search of advice, or to use your tape measure to verify legal stick lengths. Starting on time also leads to finishing on time—a not inconsiderable benefit that keeps everyone on schedule, and prevents hurried parents from becoming upset when they arrive to pick up their children and find them still practicing.

Practice Scenarios

Below are two practice session outlines. The first is a basic daily practice, suitable for all ages, which you can use as a starting point in developing your own practice schedule. The second is a "first week" schedule that covers most of what your players need to know before the season begins. These scenarios are for working with about twenty to twenty-five players, assuming the team has access to a full-size, outdoor lacrosse field with two cages. Most drill situations can be adjusted for half-field availability and a smaller-player turnout.

1. Basic Daily Practice

0:00 — 0:05 Coach Talk

With the first whistle, bring your players in and have them take a knee in front of you. Make sure you can see all of their faces and they can see and, most important, hear you. Take five minutes to discuss the team goals for the practice and what the players will be working to accomplish that day. You may want to concentrate on defensive tactics, or introduce a new play, or the team may be preparing for an upcoming game and you want a light-contact practice with emphasis on field communication. Be as direct as possible so everyone stays focused on the same objectives.

0:05 — 0:10 Warm-Up Run

Players need to loosen up and a half-speed run is a good way to do it. Form the team into one or two uniform lines, led by the captains or the day's appointed leaders, and have them circle the field two or three times at an easy pace.

0:10 — 0:20 Stretching

This is an absolute necessity for all ages to prevent injury and improve flexibility. Young players may not require it as much, but it teaches them the basics they'll need later on. Coaches should research proper stretching techniques or try to find a qualified volunteer to help (such as someone from the local schools, or a personal trainer or physical therapist related to a team member). Muscle groups that require stretching are the legs (calf, thigh, hamstring, quadriceps), lower back, groin, and shoulders.

0:20 — 0:35 Line Drills and Goalie Warm-Up

The ability to use a lacrosse stick—to catch, throw, cradle, and scoop ground balls—is the most fundamental and necessary skill in lacrosse. A player can be a genius at understanding offensive and defensive concepts, or possess unmatched athletic ability, but without well-honed stick skills he won't go far in this sport. Stickwork should be heavily emphasized during the first two weeks of the season for experienced players, and throughout the season for novices.

Groups of players, overseen by more experienced players, team captains, or assistant coaches, can be spread around the field in opposing lines to work on the throwing and catching drills described later in this book. Meanwhile, you or other assistant coaches can use this time to warm up the goalies.

Two goalies can warm up at once if two coaches and two cages are available. If only one coach is available, he can throw at the cage with one goalie defending while the other stands behind the goal and the end line backing up shots. (Note: It's not a good idea to let other players assist in this drill, as they will typically concentrate more on their own shooting than on training the goaltender.)

0:35 — 0:50 Position-Specific Drills

Break the team into groups of attack, defense, and midfield players and have them work separately on primary skills used in game situations. Attack can focus on exercises such as executing inside rolls or shooting off a pass. Middies can practice the various dodges they'll need, follow-up shots at the cage, or face-offs. Defense might work on long passes, field positioning, and footwork.

There are also position-specific drills that the team can work on together but allow players to sharpen individual skills. One-on-one drills from behind the cage and from the top of the restraining box, for example, allow midfielders and attackmen to go up against real defenders while enabling defensemen to practice their footwork and stick checks.

0:50 — 1:05 Ball Handling and Passing Drills

At the beginner level, players are just learning to keep the ball in the pocket of the stick. Simple drills such as scoop-tuck-and-cradle while running between plastic cones become second nature to game veterans, but they can be a challenge to younger players. Arrange cones in lines, squares, or zigzag patterns to create an obstacle course players need to cradle through. Emphasize switching hands, one-hand cradles, evading checks from defending players, and keeping the stick to the outside of the body away from the cones.

When not working on ball handling, bring the team together for some full-field passing drills. Variations of this drill are discussed later, but all of them stress moving the ball downfield by finding an open man on the run. As the season progresses and teams become more adept at passing and cradling, practice in this area can be scaled back or scrapped entirely.

1:05 — 1:25 Unsettled Play (Offense vs. Defense)

One of the most vital uses of practice time is concentrating on "unsettled" play in all its forms (more on this later). Lacrosse is a fast-moving sport—game scores can change quickly after turnovers, and controlling the ball means controlling the tempo of play. Exercises that focus on ground balls are essential. Fast breaks and drills simulating 5-on-4 or 3-on-2 situations should be practiced regularly, if not at every session.

1:25 — 1:35 Hodgepodge

A block of time can be dedicated to items you don't need to work on every day, but are required knowledge for games. Defining rules and regulations for situations such as offside, or demonstrating the difference between legal and illegal checks, fit in well here. You can cover infrequently used plays, such as settled rides and clears, or introduce a new offensive or defensive concept to add to the team's repertoire.

1:35 — 1:55 Settled Play

This practice period is for straight-out offense versus defense, either 6-on-6 half field or a full field scrimmage. Use this time to go over defensive slides and offensive sets and plays, tweaking and correcting as you go. Maintain a brisk pace and make replacements often. A good way to rotate is by changing a defenseman every three whistles and an attackman every four. Midfield lines can be switched after a set number of minutes, ensuring that every line plays both offensive and defensive sides of the ball.

1:55 — 2:00 Fun and Conditioning

Finish practices with something fun. One way is to have players compete to see who can score off the most creative shot, with the winner getting to sit out half the team's wind sprints. Try to end each practice session with some type of conditioning drill, but don't make it exhausting. Lacrosse is a running sport, and every player, at every age, needs to work on developing wind and stamina. Just be sure not to overwork younger players. You want to encourage effort, teach discipline, and build your team, but you'll find that more players will return to practice sessions if they go home feeling good about their efforts.

2. First-Week Practice

Here, the term "first week" is used to describe the first five consecutive practices held by a novice youth team in the beginning of the season, but not necessarily taking place in a week's time. These practices will be quite different from midseason practices, as in the beginning you'll need time to introduce yourself and your coaching style to the players and cover all of the major playing points they need to understand before they step on the field for competitive play.

Early on, you'll need to determine when and how long practice sessions should run. Try to schedule practices the same time and day of the week throughout the season. Also try to get in at least ten practices before your first game, instructing during the "first week" and then duplicating this routine and fine-tuning during the "second" week. This way, your players will have the fundamentals covered before their first game and can build on those basics for the remainder of the season.

As you and the team go through early practices you'll need to make some decisions about style of play and how to gain the most from the group you are working with. Will you run a zone defense or man-to-man style? Offensively, what type of sets will work best for your players? Should you train them for the fast break, pushing the ball quickly to goal, or a more methodical 6-on-6 style that stresses settled ball movement and plays? Your answers to these questions will depend as much as anything else on the makeup of your team and the skills of the players. For example, if you have a squad filled with track stars, your offense can capitalize on fast breaks. As you coach your players, you're also responsible for assessing their strengths and weaknesses.

Day One

This all-important first day is all about greeting your players, establishing rules, and teaching the most basic fundamentals of lacrosse. If you or your assistant coaches played lacrosse (or other sports), take a few minutes to describe your backgrounds and coaching credentials, and talk briefly about the sport itself and the object of the game.

The best place to start your instruction is at the beginning—by teaching the proper way to handle the stick. Novice players, even those with some familiarity with lacrosse, will quickly develop quirky, individual styles unless you instill, and insist on, the proper fundamentals before any bad habits take hold.

Move on to give an overview of the drills players will learn during practices, thoroughly explaining each drill, its purpose, and how players will benefit by executing them properly. Spend much of the first day's practice running line drills and generally having the players experience moving the ball around and getting used to having a lacrosse stick in their hands.

Day One Schedule

- ○ Introduce coaching staff to players
- ○ Explain team rules and expectations
- ○ Discuss practice plan for coming week
- ○ Give an introduction to warm-ups and line drills
- ○ Explain and teach basic stick fundamentals

  Teach catching

  Teach passing

  Teach cradling

  Teach scooping/ground balls

Day Two

Now that your players have at least the rudiments of stick skills, you can begin teaching them the basics of field strategy, such as getting players to recognize field "balance" and the need to fill gaps as players move, off-ball movement and getting open, and the different types of dodges and shots. This may require some "classroom" or chalkboard instruction, but it should culminate in players getting out onto the field for drills that put what they have learned into practice. Continue to spend a considerable amount of time on warm-ups and line drills.

Day Two Schedule

- ○ Warm-ups and line drills
- ○ Offensive theory

  Off-ball movement

  Picks

  Cuts

  Move and fill

  Dodges

        Face dodge

        Split dodge

        Roll dodge

        Bull dodge

○   Types of shots

        Overhand

        Sidearm

        Bounce

        Underhand

○   Dodging/shooting drills

Day Three

At this point, scale back the time spent on warm-ups and line drills, and begin focusing on defense. Start with footwork, an important part of defensive play, then move to defensive stickhandling techniques and the proper way to execute a slide. Players should also practice using the offensive moves they learned in the previous day's session.

One method you can use in teaching defensive footwork is to have players put down their sticks and defend using only their feet and bodies. Show them how to use their hands (allowed in certain circumstances) without shoving (illegal and penalized). Also teach the proper way to bodycheck, but discourage body checking in practices. In contact sports, especially among younger players, the stronger ones often find it easy to bully the smaller ones, which discourages many youths from continuing. Have them save body checking for the game.

After working on defensive skills, segue into transition play and fast breaks, tying together lessons from both the offensive and defensive playbooks.

Day Three Schedule

○   Warm-ups and line drills

○   Defensive theory

○   Defensive footwork

        Breakdown

        Drop step

        Lateral movements

- ◐ Slides
  - Crease slide
  - Adjacent slide
  - Proper slide execution
- ◐ Stick checks
  - Poke
  - Slap
  - Lift
- ◐ Unsettled play
  - Fast breaks
  - Transition offense/defense

Day Four

If two coaches are available, split the team in half, with one coach teaching defensive formations and the other offensive sets. Don't overwhelm the players at this point with details and specifics. Instead, focus on the overall concepts of each formation and set. Also, don't attempt to teach everything in one practice. One offensive and defensive game strategy is sufficient early in the season. If you find your players picking up on the concepts quickly, you can introduce more.

Select a play or two from the offensive formation and practice it, emphasizing that offense players should know what to do from every position on the field. Create handouts of play diagrams with different colors assigned to each man on the field. When a player is sent into the scrimmage he can be shown the handout and told, "Do what this color player is doing." This helps novices easily replicate field movements in the beginning without having to memorize complex plays, which they will eventually learn.

Day Four Schedule

- ◐ Warm-ups and line drills
- ◐ Defensive formations
  - Man-to-man
  - Zone
- ◐ Slides
- ◐ Offensive sets

      1–3–2 set

      1–4–1 set

      2–2–2 set

O   Introduction to offensive plays

Day Five

In the final day of the "first week," introduce riding and clearing, an important but often not well-understood aspect of the game. When the team can successfully execute this maneuver in its various forms, with players switching offensive and defensive roles, they will have completed at least a cursory yet thorough introduction to playing lacrosse.

Now you can run them through their first real, full-field scrimmage. Let the players "air it out" a bit, stopping play only when necessary to correct mistakes and make adjustments. This is a fun and exciting reward for a team that has unquestionably worked hard and learned a lot in a short amount of time.

Day Five Schedule

O   Warm-ups and line drills

O   Clearing

      Unsettled clear off shot

      Settled clear off whistle

      Sideline clear

O   Riding

      Unsettled ride off shot

      Settled zone ride off whistle

      Settled man-to-man ride off whistle

      Sideline ride

O   Full-field scrimmage

Wrapping It Up

Throughout the "first week" of practice, coaches must observe with a critical eye and take notes to keep track of aspects such as team weaknesses and which drills will continue to need improvement in certain areas. Corrections should be made in increments, not large strides. Make sure the team at least understands each concept, even if the players are still far from perfect in executing it, before moving to a more advanced stage.

Finally, always insist that players practice and play with proper fundamentals. Don't let errors slide—correct them whenever and wherever they occur. At this level, you'll be doing a disservice to your team if you do not correct mistakes early, allowing them to develop into bad habits.

Practice Expectations

Players usually want to know how they can improve their game beyond what they learn at team practices. This is something you want to encourage. Great players work very hard on their game, whether during practices or on their own free time.

The simplest, most effective, and most practical activity for becoming a better player is one that anyone can do by himself with nothing more than a stick, a ball, and a solid wall. Consistently playing wall ball for only fifteen to twenty minutes a day, every day, will produce amazing results in a player's stickhandling ability. Encourage players to try different things such as throwing and catching on the run and switching hands after each toss to create an exercise that is both fun and functional. In a similar vein, a player can find a backstop or a lacrosse goal and practice his shooting. Again, promote making this challenging and fun. Hanging aluminum cans on strings in the goal make great targets for working on accuracy.

Players should be encouraged to work on speed, agility, and weight training on their own time to supplement skills learned in practice and in play. Conditioning drills such as running (distance and sprint) and plyometrics build stamina, jumping rope improves footwork, and weight training builds muscles, which increases speed and arm strength needed to throw faster checks and harder shots.

Another practical and low-cost way to improve one's game is to watch and study collegiate teams, either in person or on tape. Even if there isn't a collegiate program nearby, more and more games are being televised nationally and there are services that offer game tapes of the elite teams for a relatively low cost. Tell your players to focus not only on their particular position and the movement of the ball itself, but how the men on the field move and react in all positions. Teach your team to pay attention to how the offense cuts or the defense slides and to emulate that correct form and replicate it in their own play. It isn't easy in the beginning, as the first reaction is to watch the game purely for enjoyment, but after some practice, studying how good teams play will help a youngster's own game.

Finally, if the financial resources are available, lacrosse camps are an excellent way to improve a young player's skills while he has a fun time doing so. Lacrosse camps are held around the country, mainly on university campuses during the summer months, and are staffed by college coaches and all-star players. The camps are a fantastic way to learn different approaches to the game from a variety of sources, to meet other players from around the country, and to build on specific weaknesses and skill sets. Camps range from general to position-focused to elite (invitation-only camps for the nation's best players). For one or two weeks players live and breathe lacrosse instruction and scrimmages, whether in an overnight or day camp structure, and camps are available for all age ranges. Just attending a camp isn't enough though. Coaches should discuss with their players before they attend what aspects of their game they should work on, and encourage them to push themselves while they are there. Camps are one of the best times for a player to experiment and add new tricks to his arsenal. Hard work and concentration may be more difficult than messing around and having fun, but it will pay off in the long run.

CHAPTER 3

FUNDAMENTALS
OF LACROSSE

The object of modern lacrosse is to score by advancing a ball into the goal of the opponent's team. The ball can be shot, bounced, batted, even kicked into the goal, but hands may not be used to touch or move the ball. Each goal counts as one point in the youth and collegiate game, regardless of how or where it was scored (in major league lacrosse, two points are awarded for shots from outside an arc line marked on the field).

Playing periods consist of four fifteen-minute quarters, for a total game time of sixty minutes. Midway between the first and second periods, and the third and fourth periods, are two-minute intervals. At halftime there is a ten-minute intermission. Playing time and intervals between periods may be altered if agreed upon by both teams prior to the match.

The team leading in score at the end of sixty minutes is declared the victor. If the score is tied at the end of regulation play, "sudden death" overtime is played (the new, politically correct term is "sudden victory") following a two-minute intermission. Periods of four minutes are played until a team scores, deciding the game winner.

Each team may have no more than ten players on the field at any given time. Teams usually consist of one goaltender, three defensemen, three attackmen, and three midfielders, although the configuration of midfielders with long or short sticks often changes according to missing-man ("man down") penalties and play strategies.

Attackmen and offensive midfielders use short sticks. Defensemen and some midfielders use longer sticks. Goaltenders have a special goalie stick, or crosse, with a wide head for blocking shots. No more than one goaltender stick and four long poles may be on the field at the same time. There is no limit to the amount of short sticks that can be used by a team during play.

Advancing the Ball

To keep the flow of the game moving, there are time restrictions on advancing the ball.

A goaltender who saves a shot within the marked circle surrounding the goal (the *crease*), or gathers a loose ball while in the crease, or receives a pass while in the crease has four seconds to move the ball out of the crease before time expires. If the ball isn't passed, or the goalie does not leave the crease area within those four seconds, the ball is awarded to the other team. Attacking players are prohibited from entering the opposing team's goal crease at any time. If a player in possession of the ball steps or deliberately leaps into the opposing team's crease, any goal that occurs is disallowed and the ball is awarded to the other team. Players are not even allowed to enter their own crease when carrying the ball, although if they gain possession of the ball while in the crease it is not a violation providing they pass the ball out or vacate the crease area within four seconds.

When a defending team gains possession of the ball within the defensive half of the field, its players are allowed twenty seconds to move the ball beyond the midfield line. Failure to clear the ball from the defensive half within the time limit will result in the ball being awarded to the other team.

When the team in possession of the ball advances across the midfield line, it has ten seconds to bring the ball into the attack area of the field. The ball can be passed or carried out of the attack area once brought in, but a new ten-second count will begin, requiring the ball to advance. Failure to advance the ball into the attack area within ten seconds after crossing the midfield line will result in the ball being awarded to the other team.

During the final two minutes of regulation play, offensive stalling rules go into effect for the team that is ahead in scoring. At the two-minute mark, the team in the lead is notified and required to "keep it in" their attack area once the ball has been brought in. If the ball is moved out of this attack area in any manner, except as a result of a shot at the goal or a deflection by a defending player, the ball will be awarded to the opposing team.

If no team is ahead in scoring with less than two minutes to play, neither team is required to "keep it in" the attack area.

Time-Outs

Each team receives four nonconsecutive time-outs per game, with no more than two allowed during each half. Unused time-outs do not carry over from the preceding halves. During sudden death overtime, one time-out is awarded to each team for each period. Time-outs can last no longer than two minutes.

During a "dead ball" situation (when time is suspended for any reason), time-out may be called by any player on the field or either team's head coach. While the ball is in play, time out only may be called by the team in possession of the ball on the offensive area of the field.

Substitutions

At any time during the course of the game, players can be substituted "on the fly." During dead ball situations, players may be substituted before a restart of play if a horn is requested. A horn can be requested by the coach if the ball goes out of bounds on the sidelines, or a time-serving penalty is enforced, stopping play. There is no horn to substitute players if a ball goes out of bounds on either end line, for non-time-serving penalties, or if play is suspended for an equipment infraction. A horn is not required for substitutions during time-outs or intermission.

Players substituting on the fly can only enter the game when the player coming off the field actually leaves the field of play. A player is not allowed to block or delay a substitute from leaving or entering the field. Players also may not enter the substitution box (at the midfield sideline in front of the scorer's table area) unless a substitution is imminent.

Offside

While in play, a team with less than three players on the offensive side of the field, or with less than four defenders on the defensive side of the field, is judged offside. A key rule change in 2001 allows fewer than four men on the defensive side if three of the team's players are in the penalty box. As long as the numbers are correct, players can move upfield and downfield freely. For example, if a midfielder remains on the defensive side of the field with his three defensemen teammates, the goaltender is allowed to move across the midfield line.

Field Layout

The lacrosse field is shaped like a football field but is slightly larger, measuring 110 yards long and 60 yards wide. In regulation games, these dimensions are mandatory—unless both teams mutually agree, in writing, to different dimensions (an important point because lacrosse is often played on nonconforming fields). It's also important because, if the dimensions can't be corrected in time for the game start and no mutual agreement has been filed with the district assignor, the home team begins the game with two penalties: a designated home player serves a three-minute, non-releasable penalty for unsportsmanlike conduct, and a second player serves a thirty-second, releasable penalty for "field not meeting specifications."

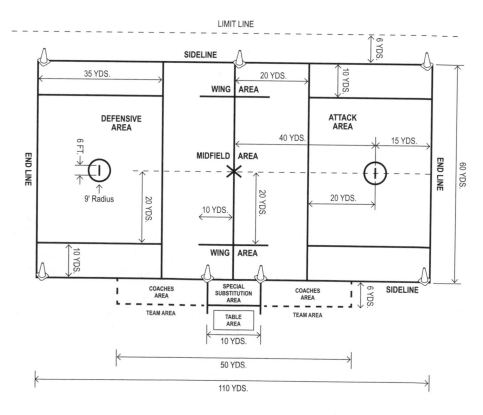

The lacrosse goal, or *cage*, is more like a hockey goal, but again incrementally larger—six feet high and six feet wide, constructed of metal pipe and consisting of two vertical posts joined by a top crossbar, with a net that prevents the ball from reentering play. A line drawn between the goalposts indicates the plane of the goal, or *goal line*. (Players often refer to an imaginary line, called the *goal line extended*, which runs from the goal line across the field to the sidelines. The GLE is a useful reference point to warn teammates of attackers coming around the crease, for positioning players around the goal, etc.) The goals, at opposite ends of the field, are centered between the sidelines and placed fifteen yards in from each end line. Around the goal is a circle with a nine-foot radius known as the *goal crease*.

Despite their similar size and shape, lacrosse fields are not marked off like football gridirons. A *center* or *midfield line* divides the lacrosse field across the middle. Two sections, the *defensive area* and *attack area*, are created by another two lines, called *restraining lines*, twenty yards out from the midfield line. A *restraining box* is created by parallel lines ten yards in from each sideline, which connect the restraining line and end line.

The midpoint of the center line is marked with an X and is designated for face-offs. Twenty yards out from this spot, *wing lines* are drawn parallel to the sidelines, extending ten yards on each side of the midfield line.

A substitution area is provided six yards off the sideline and extending five yards on each side of the center line. Only players serving penalty time, players ready to substitute on the fly, the chief bench official, and official scorers and timers are allowed in this area.

Lacrosse Equipment

Helmets

All players must wear a protective helmet fastened with a chin strap and fitted with a protective metal face mask. Standards for helmets and face masks are determined by the National Operating Committee on Standards for Athletic Equipment (NOCSAE), and players must use helmets that meet those standards.

Protective mouthpieces covering the upper teeth are also required. They must be a highly visible color and worn at all times on the field of play. Clear or colorless mouthpieces are not allowed unless an exception is granted. Any player on the field not wearing a mouthpiece or other required equipment during play is subject to a one-minute, non-releasable personal foul penalty.

Until the early 1990s, lacrosse helmets were generally uncomfortable and ill-fitting because of the few basic sizes and nearly identical styles available. They were constructed of pliable plastic sections, sewn and riveted together, with string laces in the back that allowed a player to adjust the helmet's width to conform to his head. The interior was lined with pliable foam that hardened over time, adding to the poor fit and discomfort. Face masks were strongly built but heavy, which helped to obscure a player's field of vision.

The recent, rapid growth in youth lacrosse has prompted significant advances in helmet design by a number of equipment manufacturers, giving today's players more options when it comes to choosing a helmet that is right for them. The laces used for adjusting the fit have been eliminated. Helmets are now available in many sizes and are constructed with lighter, more breathable foams and molded plastics. Some helmets include foam inserts or occipital lobe adjustment straps for optimum custom fitting. Helmets now average around two pounds in weight, with more advanced and expensive types weighing even less, without any sacrifice to the increased protection they offer. Air vents provide increased ventilation, and redesigned ear openings allow for better communication.

Face masks have been redesigned as well to improve not only the protection they offer but also for better player vision, both forward-looking and peripheral. The masks are now made of metal alloys and titanium for a greater strength-to-weight ratio. Face masks now extend lower to better protect the jawline and chin, while allowing for greater visibility below a player's line of vision.

Goalkeepers are required to wear extra protection on their helmets in the form of a throat protector. These protectors are fashioned from either hard foam or molded plastic, and attach to the chin guard at the bottom of the face mask. Some helmet types require a special throat protector that fits the unique design of their face masks, while other versions are universal and adapt to virtually any helmet. Foam throat guards are generally smaller, less expensive, and offer the least protection. Higher-quality throat protectors, especially those designed specifically for the helmet, encompass the player's neck in a shell of hard plastic and offer superior protection. Most cost almost twice as much as the least-expensive foam guards, but are exponentially more protective.

Selecting a helmet often comes down to choosing which factors are most important to each player. Some compromise may be required to find one that offers the right combination of fit, weight, vision, and price, but in the end a helmet is the one item that will be most noticeable—and could have the most significant effect on playing performance—if it isn't what the individual is comfortable with.

Body Armor

Arm pads and shoulder pads are required for all field players except the goalkeeper (who requires a special chest protector). Unlike gloves and helmets that offer different options and features based mainly on player comfort, the design of arm and shoulder pads is determined by the position played, and by each individual's need or desire for speed, flexibility, or protection.

Lacrosse shoulder pads are lightweight and flexible, protecting the vital areas of the chest without restricting arm movement.
Photo courtesy of Warrior Lacrosse

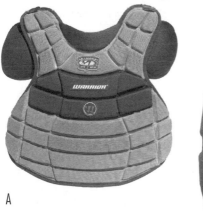

A

B

Goaltenders are required to wear specific equipment such as a chest protector (photo A) and throat guards. They may also opt to wear pants with pads sewn into them (photo B).
Photos courtesy of Warrior Lacrosse

Arm pads come in two general types: a sleeve style that slips onto the arm and uses an elastic fabric for a snug fit, or an exoskeleton style that uses Velcro straps to secure articulated sections on the upper arm and forearm. Attackmen (the primary ball-handlers and scorers on the lacrosse field) are usually opposed by long-stick defenders who use their sticks and bodies to check hard and often in order to defend their goals. As a result, many attackmen choose pads that offer maximum arm protection from the cuff of the glove all the way up to the bottom of the shoulder pad. Arm pads that have this rugged exoskeleton design are typically made of fabric with layers of interior foam under hard plastic outer shells.

Defenders, who rarely carry the ball but require mobility and speed to keep pace with the attackmen, may opt for a sleeve-style pad that is lighter and less bulky. Beginners and youth players may also find these pads to be the best option, as they are more cost effective and because younger players don't ordinarily encounter the checking strength and speed that high school and college players possess. For the player who needs only a bare minimum of protection, simple slip-on elbow pads are a good choice. They cover only the elbow cap, usually with a hard-plastic shell surrounded by foam, and allow the greatest range of movement while adhering to the rule book requirements for protective equipment.

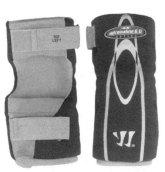

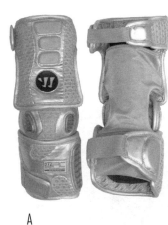

B

A

C

Players have a variety of arm pads to choose from, each offering a different level of protection suitable for different positions. Attackmen can expect repeated checks to the arms and may opt for heavier body armor (photo A). Midfielders who require protection from defenders' sticks but who also need mobility may choose somewhat lighter pads (photo B). Defenders, whose job is to check quickly and often but who are less likely to be checked themselves, typically choose minimum required protection such as elbow caps (photo C).
Photos courtesy of Warrior Lacrosse

Gloves

Lacrosse gloves used to be made entirely of stiff leather, and each section was stuffed with thick padding. The gloves were heavy, cumbersome, and allowed no feel of the stick in the hands. Because the leather was so thick, they needed to be broken in through constant use, and it could take months before they were fully conditioned. The fingers were difficult to move, and the palms tended to dry out and become rigid, further limiting and often preventing a good grip on the stick.

Today's gloves use strong, lightweight synthetic materials to offer increased protection in the thumb and wrist areas, and unlike old-style leather gloves, they require no break-in period.
Photo courtesy of Warrior Lacrosse

Along with advances to the stick itself, the evolution of lacrosse gloves has been a major reason that the ball- and stickhandling skills of the players has dramatically increased. With today's gloves, players now have better control of the stick and can handle more checks and abuse before giving up the ball. The newer gloves also provide a greater range of motion, allowing players to fake passes more easily, shoot and pass better, and cradle the ball with amazing ability.

Players today have a wide selection of gloves to choose from, suitable for every budget or need. Most lacrosse equipment manufacturers offer upward of six types of gloves, ranging from the most basic and inexpensive cloth models for beginners to state-of-the-art professional leather gloves sporting the very latest innovations in comfort and protection. Modern gloves do not require a break-in period, and computer-engineered design allows them to function much like the human hand itself. Most styles mimic the way the fingers bend, with padding divided into different sections for unmatched flexibility. High-end gloves contain moisture-wicking fabrics and vent holes that keep hands dry and cool. Some gloves have textured palms for an improved grip. Split or "floating" wrist cuffs offer greater protection and ball-cradling movement, while gel padding improves impact absorption and disperses shock. Goalies may want gloves that offer added protection to the thumbs, with hard-plastic shells and foam tips that protect against direct ball shots. These gloves offer superior protection, but at the cost of some flexibility and weight.

Altering gloves to improve their grip is not permitted under NOC-SAE rules. Cutting out sections of leather, a practice known as "palming" the gloves, renders them unusable in a regulation game. Players who wear gloves that have been altered will receive a non-releasable, one-minute personal foul penalty. Gloves that are worn through, with holes in the palms, may be used if the holes are not too large or if they are taped or sewn. Gloves also can be repalmed professionally by lacrosse specialty stores.

Footwear

The choice of footwear a player uses will depend mainly on the field surface. Lacrosse is traditionally played on grass, but artificial surfaces are becoming more common. Standard molded cleats are the norm for grass and field turf surfaces. Removable cleats are allowed, but by rule cleat length cannot exceed one-half inch. For artificial turf fields, running shoes or special turf shoes can be worn. These turf shoes have a softer sole than cleats, but do not have spikes because there is nothing to dig into. Instead, they are covered with rubber studs to improve traction.

Crosse

The stick, or *crosse* as it is properly (and officially) known, is an extension of each player, and tends to become a very personal item. Various models and types are available, and each crosse can be adjusted in a number of ways to conform to a player's desires, whether for better ball handling, increased shot speed, pocket depth for ease of catching, or even reduction of weight. As such, the crosse is also the most heavily regulated item in the game.

A crosse consists of two parts: a *head* (usually plastic), which contains the *pocket*, and a metal or wood *shaft*. Offensive players use a short crosse and defensemen use a long crosse. No more than four long crosses are allowed on the field at any given time, but there is no minimum number required. There is no limit to the number of players carrying short sticks on the field, and no regulations governing players using a long stick to face-off or play offense.

The total length of the crosse is fixed at forty to forty-two inches for the short crosse or fifty-two to seventy-two inches for the long crosse. The head at its widest point must measure a minimum of six and one-half inches from sidewall to sidewall, and a minimum of ten inches, inside measurement, from top to bottom. The goalkeeper's crosse can be as short as forty inches or as much as seventy-two inches in length. Its head can vary from ten to twelve inches at its widest point. All sticks must have a ball-stop at the base of the head that is wide enough to permit the ball to move freely. All stick shafts must have a cap or plug on the exposed end, or must be adequately taped to prevent injury.

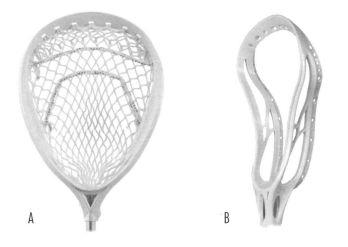

A   B

Lacrosse sticks are the most closely regulated equipment in the game. Goalies are allowed to use a stick with a much larger head and pocket (photo A); a typical player stick head (photo B) is smaller and slimmer by comparison.
Photos courtesy of Warrior Lacrosse

Innovations to the crosse, both heads and shafts, have had a dramatic impact on the game. The original lacrosse sticks were made of wood and leather, weighed as much as five pounds, and were hand-made—giving each a unique feel and temperament.

As effective as wood crosse shafts were, they had many shortcomings. They were easily broken in hard play, which often resulted in player injuries. Wood is also slippery and hard to grip, especially when wet, so players would wind them with tape, which only increased their already considerable weight. As new, improved materials became available, the crosse shaft moved from wood to more durable but heavier aluminum, and then to lighter-weight graphite, and finally to even stronger, lighter titanium. These changes revolutionized the game. They made the sticks increasingly easier to handle, allowing defensemen to throw lightning-fast checks and attackers to hurl the ball at amazing speeds. Less expensive metal alloy combinations also have been developed, reducing the cost of the shafts and in some cases actually reducing their weight, while still maintaining a high strength-to-weight ratio. Stick handles now also come textured, improving their grip without the use of tape.

In the early 1970s, plastic heads appeared, offering consistency in durability, design, and feel. In 1994, Brine introduced the first offset head (previously, all heads were in straight alignment with the shaft). By dropping the head below the centerline of the shaft, the leverage of the throw increased, augmenting ball speed. This offset also allowed for better ball retention in the pocket. Nearly all crosse heads made today use this design.

The pocket of the crosse can be strung in a variety of ways. Manufacturers offer a wide array of pocket designs and stick heads with attachment holes in unique positions to allow for a diversity of stringing styles. There is no right or wrong style—players generally choose whatever they are most comfortable using. Coaches should work with players to determine which pocket style is best for each and encourage players to experiment with different styles off the field.

The two basic pockets are traditional and mesh. Traditional styles have leather or synthetic strips interwoven with string, creating an open, diamondlike basket pattern. Traditional pockets require more break-in time and maintenance, requiring restringing when the strings or supporting strips break. Because leathers are susceptible to moisture, a soggy day can have a noticeable effect and actually change the dynamics of the pocket, throwing the entire crosse completely out of whack. However, this setup allows for a better feel of the ball, and players generally choose the traditional pocket for its ball-handling characteristics.

Stringing Options Different types of stringing styles are permitted, providing the pockets conform to the size and shape dictated by the rules. The first stick has a hard mesh pocket with double inverted "V" shooting strings. The second has a wide-hole mesh that is lighter and more flexible than hard mesh. The third stick has traditional stringing with leather thongs. The stick at far right has a soft mesh pocket with basic horizontal shooting strings.

Mesh pockets use a single piece of woven fabric attached to the stick head, and the mesh itself is available in a variety of styles. Players can opt for a softer or stiffer mesh, or a mesh with larger or smaller spacing, depending on their preference. Mesh pockets are less affected by changes in weather and are easy to adjust and maintain, making them a practical and dependable choice, especially for novice players. Mesh pockets also can be quickly replaced by following the provided instructions, while restringing a traditional pocket takes some skill and practice.

The rule book has many notations that address the size, shape, and design of stick pockets. A pocket is too deep if the top surface of the lacrosse ball rests below the bottom edge of the sidewall. Pockets are not allowed to be strung in any way that makes it difficult for an opponent to dislodge the ball, or for the player to withhold the ball from play—when the crosse is rotated ninety degrees, the ball should be able to roll out of the head unhindered. All trailing strings and leathers are limited to a length of six inches.

A pocket that sags or is strung so that the ball rests below the sidewalls of the stick head (top photo) is illegal and will draw a penalty. The bottom photo shows a correctly strung pocket.
Photos courtesy of Ron Dubé Design

As noted, a crosse may be tailored to some degree to suit individual playing styles, but it must also be pointed out that there are tricks players sometimes use to alter a crosse that the rule book does not allow. Such methods include pinching the head to narrow the sidewalls, either by simply bending it or by heating the plastic and "baking" the head. Another trick is to shave or sand the sidewalls to make them thinner and more flexible. Adding extra ball stops to retain the ball also gives unfair advantage.

Any player caught using an illegal stick is subject to a one-minute or three-minute non-releasable penalty, depending on the severity of the offense, and the stick can be removed for the duration of the game. For example, a pocket that has sagged too deep will draw a one-minute non-releasable penalty, but the player may adjust the stick and return to the game with it. On the other hand, a player found using a stick that is too short, or one that has a pinched head, will serve a three-minute non-releasable penalty and the offending stick will remain at the scoring table area for the remainder of the game.

During each half, the officials will select one player from each team, usually someone who has scored or frequently handles the ball, and inspect that player's equipment and stick. In addition, during the course of the game any coach can request one "free check" of a specific player's equipment and crosse without incurring a penalty. If a coach makes a second or subsequent request, and all equipment is found to be legal, the request team will be charged a time-out or technical foul if no time-outs remain. Goals scored in a game will count if a stick is later found to be illegal; however, if an equipment-check request is made *after* a goal but *before* the whistle for the following face-off, and the stick is found to be illegal, the goal will be waived off.

The position of the players usually determines the type of stick that they use. Offensive attackmen and midfielders wield a short stick, which is better suited for ball handling, passing, and shooting. These players typically cut their sticks as short as allowed, leaving less of it vulnerable for a defender to hit and making the stick as light as possible. Among the variety of heads to choose from, offensive players may want a head that is ultralight, and narrower in the sidewall design. Defensemen carry a long stick, almost six feet in length, which gives them the reach and leverage they need to make checks and keep an offensive player at a good distance. Defenders usually prefer stiffer, wider stick heads that are more effective for checking and knocking down passes, mated to a rugged, lightweight titanium or alloy shaft for increased check speed.

When is the right time (age) for a defensive player to start using a long stick? The rule of thumb that should always be observed is that the long stick should never be taller than the player himself. But with children getting into the game of lacrosse at earlier ages than ever before, the question of when a long stick is appropriate is being debated around the country, and youth programs are adopting a rule that prohibits the player's shaft size to be no longer than forty inches until he plays in seventh grade. There is no question that the long stick is an integral part of lacrosse. With new stick technologies and the speed and skill levels of current offensive players, defensemen need the advantage of a longer stick for added leverage and checking reach. Generally though, players at this age are just mastering the basic skills of the sport, and players younger than seventh-grade age do not need to use a long stick. Although there are those who do not believe in this rule, it is my belief that younger players will benefit and actually become better defenders by using a short stick in the early part of their lacrosse careers.

Within rule book limits, stick lengths may vary based on the needs and playing styles of individuals, but as a rule of thumb long-stick length should not exceed the height of the player using it. *Photo courtesy of Ron Dubé Design*

The benefit in starting with a short stick at defense is that you never become dependant on your long pole. The long stick is a useful tool for throwing checks and maintaining distance between the player and his opponent, but true defense comes from properly using the feet and positioning the body in relation to the opponent, the ball, and the goal. All too often, a player will use the advantage of a long stick as a crutch, easily stripping novice offensive players. Unfortunately, when the offense does improve and can hold on to the ball better, the defenseman is left lacking the footwork and positioning knowledge to defend the goal, relying instead on desperate checks that will end with him being beaten or in the penalty box.

Using a short stick in the formative years will also be a benefit for stickhandling with the off-side or weak hand. A six-foot pole is unwieldy at that young age before a player has the strength to handle it properly. A beginning player will favor his strong hand, not only because of the stick's weight, but honestly, because he doesn't want to look foolish dropping balls in front of his teammates. At that rate, a player will never properly learn to use both hands. In the defensive area, good stick skills are essential. A dropped ball can quickly turn into a turnover goal. By starting with a short pole, a young player can expand his stick skills in the same manner as the offensive players, mastering not only throwing and catching, but cradling and shooting as well, all while learning the footwork and positioning of the defensive set, giving that child all the skills and confidence he needs to succeed.

CARING FOR EQUIPMENT

A crosse is each player's most valuable piece of equipment, and coaches should emphasize the importance of maintaining it in top playing condition. After use, the mesh pocket should be cleaned of mud and grass and stored where it can dry naturally to prevent the strings from stiffening. A ball or wadded newspaper placed in the pocket will help to maintain its shape. After it dries, a player may need to work the pocket back into shape by practicing with it before he takes it into a game.

Sticks can develop problems from pocket shrinkage, hard use, and a variety of other reasons. A misshapen pocket, for example, can cause a whip, which occurs when the ball hangs up or fails to exit the pocket smoothly during a pass or shot. To fix a whip:

- First, try tightening the pocket. A pocket that is too deep will cause the ball to impact the shooting strings (the strips that reinforce and stiffen the pocket) upon release. Start by adjusting the sidewalls; if that doesn't work, move to the leathers or, in the case of mesh, the string at the bottom of the pocket. Tightening the pocket will create a more gradual curve and smoother release.

CARING FOR EQUIPMENT

continued...

- Loosening the shooting strings is the next potential solution. If they are too tight the ball typically "hooks" off-target on release.

- If the above remedies fail, try adding another shooting string farther down in the pocket, which provides better stability and creates a more gradual slope, allowing the ball to roll out more easily.

Coaches should encourage players who own their sticks to keep two identical sticks at the ready for each game and practice. Even plastic heads and titanium shafts can break, and a player — or team — without reliable backup equipment is at a disadvantage.

Finally, every coach and player should know the rules regarding stick legality, and obey them. Like the proverbial lost horseshoe nail that ultimately led to a kingdom's demise, a three-minute non-releasable penalty for an illegal stick at a crucial moment could cost you a goal, a game, or even a championship.

CHAPTER 4

ESSENTIAL PLAYER SKILLS

Like many sports, lacrosse is a fast and physical team game. What sets lacrosse apart, what gives it its unique popularity, is the use of the crosse in play. But the same stick that makes this sport so fascinating to follow also can make it very frustrating to play.

The first thing any student of the game must understand is that no one is born a phenomenal lacrosse player. Unlike baseball, basketball, or football that use catching and throwing skills most people already possess, lacrosse requires the use of an instrument, an extension of the body, to accomplish these feats. As a result, lacrosse can be difficult to play, especially at the outset. And a player without adequate stick skills can't progress to the finer points of the game if the basics of catching, throwing, and cradling still elude him. Young players may develop incorrect or bad habits and find these difficult to break if they continue using them for too long. It is important that young players start off with the proper fundamentals, and the earlier they start, the more at home they will feel with a stick in their hands, allowing them to move beyond simple maneuvers to the game's more advanced concepts.

Proper fundamentals are not difficult to teach, but lacrosse requires practice, practice, practice before a player learns to instinctively catch and throw. From the start, novice lacrosse players must be drilled in manipulating the crosse with both hands, catching and throwing with the left and right. By practicing the fundamentals with both hands, a player will develop his "strong" and "off" hands equally, and will have less tendency to favor one or the other. A player who can go left or right naturally will find the sport open up for him, making him a more versatile athlete. Coaches need to emphasize these fundamentals to turn novice players into skilled attackmen and defensemen.

Finally, games are not the time when players should attempt to debut their newest moves or checks. During games, a team depends on each player understanding his position and his role on the field. Each man must "play within himself" during games and know his limitations. Coaches and players alike need to remember that practice and individual workouts are the times to try new plays or work on those special shots.

Stickhandling

The first step in catching and throwing is learning how to properly hold the crosse—gently yet firmly in both hands, with fingers and thumbs curled around the shaft and positioned to maintain balance and control. Players need to maintain a strong grip so opposing players can't knock the stick out of their hands, but the crosse should not be clutched in a tight, closed-fist grip. If the stick is held too tightly against the palms, a player's arms and hands are restricted in their movements, and the crosse will be rigid and unyielding.

Lacrosse players should always, with rare exceptions, keep both hands on the stick. Whether checking, catching, throwing, or scooping ground balls, a one-hand grip is a liability for two reasons: it could draw a penalty if a check is thrown (more on this later), and it can be more easily knocked loose in hard play.

Generally, the bottom hand on the crosse stays on the butt end of the stick—keeping the butt end covered keeps it from becoming a target for checking. This bottom hand provides support and a countermovement necessary for catching and throwing. The top hand, which controls the movement of the stick, is gripped somewhat looser, allowing it to easily move up and down the shaft as needed.

Long-pole players use different styles for catching and throwing simply because there is so much more stick to work with. A mistake that beginning players typically make is to choke up on a long stick, keeping the top hand close to the crosse head and the bottom hand in the middle of the shaft. This offers more control while catching, eliminating

An unprotected or "uncovered" stick butt offers an easy target to an opponent's checks (left). Positioning one hand low on the shaft provides better stick control and greater protection from checks (right).
Photo courtesy of Ron Dubé Design

some of the margin of error that comes with using a six-foot-long stick to intercept a ball moving at 70 mph. But a gain of control, in this case, means a loss of advantage. With one hand firmly fixed at the butt end of the shaft, a player can fully employ the benefits of a long stick, such as being able to catch a ball thrown too high, getting an advantage on a ground ball, or using maximum leverage to easily pass a ball across or downfield. Not choking up also eliminates the extra foot or two of exposed shaft below the bottom hand, which is easy for a defending player to check against someone who is running, catching, or throwing.

Coaches should instruct defending players to always carry and wield their stick above waist height. Its long length can easily cause a tripping penalty.
Photo courtesy of Dave Adams Photos

Catching

When catching the ball, players should give the thrower—their teammate—a target to aim at. A good practice tip is to hold the stick head level with the helmet, about a foot to the side and a little bit forward. When taking the shot, the catcher must try to keep the stick upright and as tight to his body as possible to make himself less vulnerable to defenders. A proper catching stance also positions him for an immediate quick-stick shot, and provides the motion needed to naturally cradle the ball and roll away from a defender.

When catching, receiving players should give their teammates a target to aim at. Coaches can instruct players to position the stick head within an imaginary "box" slightly wider than the shoulders and extending from the top of the shoulder pads to the top of the helmet.
Photo courtesy of Ron Dubé Design

When catching, a player wants to meet the ball in the air and let the stick recoil a bit to absorb the force of the throw, allowing the top hand to yield backward slightly while the bottom hand pushes forward. Lacrosse balls are very hard and move very fast. The head and pocket will flex, but unless there is some "give" with the catch, the ball will rebound out of the pocket. Catching the ball in the heart of the netting cushions the force of the throw and provides the greatest amount of surrender for the ball.

Players should always be in motion while catching, even if just taking a few steps. Standing flat-footed is a good way to lose focus, which leads to dropped balls or easy takeaways by more aggressive defenders. By moving to the ball, the player controls the moment and point of contact—which helps avoid having to handle an underthrown ball at his feet, or a ball thrown to the off-stick side of his body (the side opposite the stick head).

When catching a pass (left), allow the stick head to gently "give" with the ball (right). The slight recoil will help to retain the ball in the pocket. Instruct players to avoid using the stick to snatch or grab at the ball, which can have the opposite result. *Photos courtesy of Ron Dubé Design*

Beginning players tend to "snatch" at the ball, grabbing it from the air instead of taking the catch. This is a bad habit for a number of reasons. First, it increases the risk of the ball impacting the plastic frame of the head, causing a miss or loss of control of the ball. Second, grabbing at the ball takes a player out of his controlled "ready" position, which strips away his option for a quick-stick shot or cradle-and-roll move. Finally, a stick waving in the air is simply more vulnerable to checks.

Coaches need to drill players on catching the ball with their body between their stick and the nearest defender, which prevents the defender from blocking the shot or getting a good check on their stick (the same applies for passing—good technique is to always pass using the "outside" hand). Often, a player's best option when catching is to "roll off" and pivot away from the defender as soon as the ball hits his stick pocket, turning his back to the opponent and protecting his stick.

Throwing

After time, throwing with a lacrosse stick becomes second nature, with the body and mind performing infinite calculations to deliver the ball at a high velocity at just the right distance, hitting a one-square-foot moving target. For the beginning player, this level of competence may seem a lifetime away.

A lacrosse ball should be passed with speed and accuracy. Lob passes that float to a target take too long to arrive, and by then the defender may be in position to intercept it or meet the pass with a check. Also, players must learn to *lead* the intended target, throwing slightly ahead of the receiver—to where the player will be, not where he is when the ball is thrown. A well-thrown pass meets the receiving player where he can catch it without breaking stride.

Players practicing throwing with a lacrosse stick should follow the fundamentals and not attempt to adjust their style to the crosse. If their fundamentals are sound but their shot isn't working, they can try making adjustments to the crosse. For example, if the shooting strings are too tight, the ball may catch in the pocket or eject with a whiplike action, causing the ball to be thrown into the ground. Instead of changing the way he throws, the player may simply need to adjust the shooting strings. Remember that the crosse is just a tool, and it will require adjustments over time.

Throwing with a lacrosse stick requires practice and a certain amount of technique. Draw the shoulders and arms back to pass (left), then snap the stick forward with an overhand motion. The low hand firmly grips the butt-end of the stick while the top hand slides down the shaft. Follow-through is critical for accuracy. As shown here (right), at the end of the motion the right arm is fully extended and the right hand and stick head should be pointing toward the target.
Photo courtesy of Ron Dubé Design

Throwing with a lacrosse stick is a lesson in physics. The stick acts like a lever, with the bottom hand serving as the fulcrum. By sliding the top hand down the shaft while pushing forward, as the bottom hand is pulled toward the body, the ball is released with a sharp snap. At the end of this motion, the stick head should be pointing at the target. If the top hand grips too tightly, or does not move at all, the ball will float out of the pocket with no velocity—a lob pass. Beginning players often push or "shovel" the ball out of the crosse this way by forcing the top hand forward without the sliding movement. This prevents that sharp, whip-like action of the stick that a good pass requires.

Wall Ball Drill

The only way to improve passing and throwing skills is through practice. Wall ball is an effective exercise for both novice and experienced players, and it's a drill anyone can do on his own with just a stick, a ball, and a solid wall. A windowless wall at least ten feet high that can withstand the weight and power of a hurled lacrosse ball, such as the side of a school building or a local handball court, is ideal. Performing this exercise twenty to thirty minutes a day will help develop the hand-eye coordination, response speed, and ball-handling skills that every player needs to be proficient.

For the basic exercise, a player stands three to five yards from the wall and throws the ball at the wall, catches the rebound and cradles it once, then repeats. After thirty repetitions throwing with the right hand, the player then switches and does thirty reps throwing with the left hand. The action should become fluid and smooth—throw, catch, cradle, throw, and so on. This drill works wonders for getting new or younger players used to the feel of catching and releasing the ball. As their skills increase, players can stand closer to the wall, which not only quickens their responses, but also maximizes the number of repetitions they can do in a given time.

Basic Wall Ball Exercises

After players become familiar with the basics of wall ball, they can move on to more advanced drills, switching hands and throwing fakes as part of the drill. Players can test their consistency by building up to fifty repetitions without missing or dropping the ball, starting the count over if they miss. When players are able to complete fifty reps without interruption, they are ready for more challenging wall ball exercises.

Basic Drills

1. Single-handed throw, catch, cradle, and throw.
2. Two-handed throw, catch, cradle, and throw.
3. Using two hands, throw and catch right then throw and catch left, switching stick hands with each repetition.
4. Two-handed throw, catch, fake, and throw.

Exercise 1—Quick Stick

Stand fifteen feet from the wall. This exercise must be done quickly. Throw and catch the ball as it comes off the wall but do not cradle it—immediately send the ball back to the wall in one motion. Start with fifty right-hand throws, followed by fifty with the left. As your timing improves, move closer to the wall to work on speed, accuracy, and ball-handling skills.

Exercise 2—The Long Pass

Move back from the wall about ten yards. Throw the ball so that it returns on one bounce. Catch, cradle, and throw again. Do fifty repetitions with each hand. Work on accuracy and grabbing balls on the bounce.

Exercise 3—Passing on the Move

The point of this exercise is to improve throwing and catching skills while on a dead run, and at the same time strengthen off-stick skills. With the stick in the right hand, start at the left end of a wall, about five to ten yards out, then run parallel to the wall while throwing and catching the ball without breaking stride. As the ball rebounds, it will frequently return to the off-stick side, which requires the player to catch cross-hand. Repeat this drill with the left hand by running back from the opposite end of the wall.

Cradling

Touch and feel are important when carrying the ball in lacrosse. Although the crosse has a net pocket, the pocket is shallow and the ball can't sink into it and stay there, especially when a player is running at top speed while defensemen are trying to knock it away. The only way to maintain possession of the ball is to *cradle* it—that is, move the crosse in a rocking motion so that centrifugal force retains the ball in the pocket. A good cradling motion will prevent a player from losing the ball while executing quick, sudden moves, even if checked.

Cradling is done with the fingers, wrist, and forearm. If you break it down it looks like this: wrap the top hand around the shaft, with the stick resting where fingers meet the palm. Now slowly close the hand as if making a fist. The stick rolls inside the hand as the fingers close. Combine this action with a back-and-forth movement of the wrist, and then with a smooth back-and-forth movement of the forearm. The ball in the pocket should feel like it is sitting squarely in the middle of the head. The bottom hand maintains the balance, but it is not gripping the stick. That hand protects the stick but does not interfere with the motion of the top hand.

The harder you cradle, the more centrifugal force is exerted, making the ball feel heavier in the stick. This type of hard cradling is the *power cradle*, and it helps a player retain the ball even when blasting downfield or dodging through opponents.

Short-stick offensive players often use the *one-handed cradle*. The same motion is involved but the bottom hand no longer provides support. The stick is held almost vertically, and a sweeping arc motion is needed to retain the ball. A player may use his off-stick arm to block or protect against a defender's stick, but that arm must remain stiff and immobile. The ball carrier may not use his free arm to push away, hold on to, or redirect the check of an opposing player. This *warding off* is a technical foul that results in loss of possession.

While in possession of the ball, a player is allowed to use his arm and hand to block an opponent, but only if the arm is held immobile. If the ball carrier attempts to hold or even push away the opponent's stick, he will be flagged for "warding off" and ball possession will be awarded to the other team.

Photo courtesy of Ron Dubé Design

A player carrying the ball may not hold the crosse against his body to prevent the ball from being dislodged, or use his glove hand to grasp any part of the stick head, or "thumb" the ball to hold it in the pocket. This constitutes illegally withholding the ball from play, a technical foul, and it awards possession of the ball to the opposing team.

Younger players sometimes twirl or "spin" the stick while cradling, which can be a difficult habit to break. While not illegal, spin-cradling

"Thumbing" a ball to retain it in the stick pocket is illegal and will draw a turnover penalty.
Photo courtesy of Ron Dubé Design

puts the ball carrier at a disadvantage because his hands are not gripping the stick, and a check can easily take the ball away—and his crosse as well. Even if the ball isn't knocked away, spinning reduces a player's control of his crosse, making him unable to pass or shoot on a split-second notice.

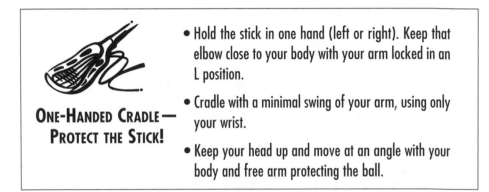

ONE-HANDED CRADLE— PROTECT THE STICK!

- Hold the stick in one hand (left or right). Keep that elbow close to your body with your arm locked in an L position.

- Cradle with a minimal swing of your arm, using only your wrist.

- Keep your head up and move at an angle with your body and free arm protecting the ball.

Scooping and Ground Balls

Ground balls lead to transitions, and the team that scores the most transition goals usually wins the game. This is especially true at the younger level, when catching and throwing aren't automatic and the ball finds itself on the field as much as in the stick. By controlling the ground ball game, your team controls the time of possession and dictates the tempo of play. Ground balls lead to fast breaks, turnovers in the offensive and defensive sides of the field, and possibly a heads-up goal if grabbed in front of the crease. Ground balls are as much about team hustle as they are method, but players skilled in the fundamental techniques of scooping will have the edge.

A few rare and gifted individuals know it instinctively, but most players need to learn that the key to fielding ground balls is to anticipate where the ball will be when they are in position to grab it. The movement and bounce of a ball are predictable, and are usually determined by factors such as the speed the ball is traveling and the type of field being played on:

- ◐ **Astroturf,** a very thin artificial surface, has a hard feel almost like industrial carpeting; it offers little resistance, so balls bounce high and roll far and fast.

- ◐ **Artificial grass,** with its imitation grass blades, functions more like natural turf, but balls tend to bounce true because the field is uniform in grade and has no underlying imperfections.

- ◐ **Natural grass fields,** even those that are meticulously maintained, have uneven dips and divots, rocks, and bare or thick patches that have more of an effect on the ball.

A stick held at too steep an angle when scooping a ball can cause it to jam into the turf (above left). To avoid this, keep the butt end of the stick low (above). The third photo (left) shows the proper form for ground ball scooping.
Photo courtesy of Ron Dubé Design

Experience teaches a player to "read" the field and the way the ball travels on it. Anticipating the actions of the ball and being prepared for any situation gives alert players a crucial jump on opponents.

While an ability to read the ball is important, good body position is essential to successful playmaking. A lower stance not only makes it easier to scoop with a crosse, it also lowers the body's center of gravity, which improves balance and makes the player a smaller target to defenders hoping to intercept him.

Players should be instructed to grip the stick firmly in both hands and "run through" the ball as they scoop it up, building momentum and speed, then immediately cradle and tuck the stick in toward their body while moving away from pressuring opponents. Players who stop to retrieve a ball, or try to "rake" it into their crosse, make themselves targets for defenders. One-handed pickups are also to be discouraged—this is lazy play, and it often results in players pushing the ball along the ground instead of picking it up into the pocket. A player using one hand to scoop the ball also tends to stand more upright, offering attackers an opportunity for a hit.

Keep your bottom hand low when scooping up a ground ball. This prevents too steep an angle with the stick, which will jam into the ground instead of getting under the ball. If a ball is too close to be picked up by running through it, or you're surrounded by other players, kick the ball out to an empty area, then run through the loose ball and pick it up. Position your stick in front of you and use your body to block out defenders; this keeps your stick out of harm's way, and if you misplay the ball or it takes a funny bounce, it will often hit your feet or torso, bouncing back to where you can play it instead of rolling behind you.

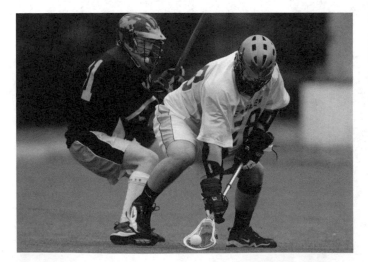

When a player positions his body between an opponent and a ground ball, he creates the protection needed to scoop up the ball without interference. *Photo courtesy of Dave Adams Photos*

If you know there are defenders chasing you, do not stop moving when you pick up a ground ball—keep running. Head for an open area where there are no opponents, which will give you time to get complete control of the ball and protect your stick. If you make a turn after scooping up a ground ball, always turn toward your bottom hand on the stick. This keeps the more vulnerable head of the stick away from any defenders who may be behind you.

Successful play depends on making the right moves. When scooping a ground ball (above left), players should be taught to turn toward their bottom hand (on the butt of the stick) to protect the stick and deny opponents an opportunity to check. In the second photo (above), the player incorrectly turns toward his top hand, exposing the stick head and ball to an opponent behind him. The third photo (left) shows the player turning the opposite way, which lets him use his body to protect the stick and block the check.
Photo courtesy of Ron Dubé Design

Picking up a loose ball is every player's mission, but if a teammate has a better chance than you of garnering the ball, and you are within five yards, the rules allow you to block out any opponents to give your teammate a clear run at the ball. This is the *man/ball* call. By yelling "Man!" you let your teammate know that you will run interference for him. The "man" player can then bodycheck and bump out a defender, but is not allowed to hold an opponent in place. This play can only be done within five yards of the ball—otherwise, interference or an illegal body check will be called.

This sequence shows two teammates, in dark jerseys, communicating and coordinating their movements to capture a loose ball while blocking out an opponent. As the three players approach the ball (left), the teammates call "Man" or "Ball" to alert each other as to what they intend to do. The player who calls "Ball" runs to pick up the loose ball while the other moves to block his "Man" (right).
Photo courtesy of Ron Dubé Design

When you are defending and attempting to stop a player ahead of you from scooping a ground ball, use your stick to poke or lift the bottom hand of the scooping player. If timed properly, this will prevent the player from capturing the loose ball, and may even cause him to run right past it, turning the play to your advantage.

Offensive and Defensive Guidelines

Over the years, lacrosse has evolved to the point that specialty players, positions, and teams play offense or defense exclusively. But this level of sophistication often does not extend to high school, intramural, or club teams, where players find themselves on the offense one minute, then must quickly switch to defense as ball possession shifts. For many players, learning offense and defense are one in the same. Even for those who play on specialty teams, knowing what an opponent is thinking—and planning—can provide a much-needed advantage.

Offensive Moves

Pick—This move is positioning your body to block or impede an opponent's movement or path. The player executing a pick must be stationary if contact is made with the opponent, otherwise it is considered a moving pick, which is illegal. The pick may not hold or continue to block out an opponent by moving to oppose him (an interference call), unless the ball is within five yards. It is also illegal for a player who is being picked to run over or knock down a stationary player.

In setting a pick, the player generally wants to deceive his opponent (a pick is not much good if the opponent knows it is coming). Rookie players tend to telegraph their picks to the other team, moving obviously and slowly. While speed and deception are necessary, the player needs to give himself adequate time to get into position and stop moving in order to catch his opponent off guard.

Because the player who sets the pick must be motionless when contact is made, it is up to the player coming off the pick—that is, a teammate the player is blocking for—to get as close as possible without being affected as well. By brushing shoulder to shoulder past the blocking player, at full speed, the teammate coming off the pick has a better chance of losing his man and allowing the pick to be successful.

When executing a pick to block for a teammate (left), the player setting the pick must remain perfectly still, with feet planted, before his opponent makes any contact with him. The player coming off the pick should run as close as possible past his immobile teammate (right) to lead his opponent into the pick.
Photos courtesy of Ron Dubé Design

Pass and pick away—One of the foundations of this sport is also one of the most underused. Off ball movements (that is, when players are not in possession of the ball) allow players to get into the open, away from defenders, so they can safely receive ball "feeds" and take shots. Picks are a tremendous asset in lacrosse for executing plays and freeing up those players. Unlike basketball, players should not pick *toward* the ball carrier, but in the opposite direction—picking *away*. After passing to the left, an offensive player would run to his right, looking for a teammate he can set a pick for. If that teammate comes off the pick successfully, he is usually in a good position to receive a pass.

V-cut—This movement is one of the best ways to get away from a tightly defending player, to free up space, or to get into position for a pass. The V-cut is so uncomplicated that it is frequently overlooked by younger players. Novice players tend to run in circles trying to get open, tiring themselves out while running again and again into their defenders. By learning the V-cut, players can employ a purposeful move they can use to get open whenever they need. Simply, the V-cut is what it sounds like: a player being blanketed by a defender can lose him by making a run toward the goal, then abruptly cutting back in the direction he started. The defender has to follow his man but will be caught unaware when the player cuts back. This move is good for at least three yards of separation.

Dodges—This is a general term for the evasive moves players make while in possession of the ball. Players should have a clear intention of what they are trying to achieve before they make a dodge. The goal of any dodge is to free up your hands in order to pass or shoot, not to juke an opponent out of his shoes. The best place to dodge is from the middle top of the restraining box, where defenders have the most difficulty cutting off the ball carrier's shooting angles. Players should avoid dodging "east to west" (left-right lateral movements that burn up energy and don't gain ground on your opponent). Work to move forward when dodging—always move toward the objective.

Developing stickhandling skills with both right and left hands is crucial for successful dodging. A player who can shoot and pass with either hand is a real threat because he can dodge at will, whereas a player with only one strong hand will have trouble getting free of opponents. For example, a right-handed player with weak left-hand skills will be forced to dodge to the right every time. It usually takes only a few attempts before defenders catch on and begin to overplay his strong side.

Players must learn to protect their stick *before and after* executing a dodge. Opponents are typically close when a ball carrier is dodging—usually just a step away from a solid stick check. To prevent losing the ball, the offensive player must keep the stick tucked close to the body until ready to pass or shoot. When releasing the ball, quick, tight movements are recommended. A "hanging" stick is an easy target for a trailing opponent.

When shooting off the dodge, especially from the midfield position, it is important to have a good shooting angle. A dodge that begins ten to fifteen yards from the outside of the nearest goalpost (or *pipe*) can put running room between a ball carrier and the defenders, allowing him to increase speed and create an "alley" or lane where he can set up the shot from an optimum angle.

Also, players should keep their heads up when they dodge. Often, players focus so intently on making a move that they spend more time watching their feet than watching what is happening on the field around them. When this happens, even if they execute a great move, they may miss a cutting teammate—or worse, a sliding defender who levels them before they can prepare for impact. Coaches can teach players to keep their heads up in to practice by standing near the top of the crease and holding up different numbers of fingers, requiring players to call out the correct number while performing a requisite dodge.

Finally, dodges must be executed at running speed to be effective. A player who isn't moving at speed will be easy to defend, or he will give an opponent time to catch up even after a successful dodge.

Face dodge—This is an easy dodge to learn and a good starting point for novice players. While running toward a defender, the ball carrier first fakes a shot or pass. The player then moves the stick across his body and face without changing hands, tucking it by his opposite ear and exploding past the opponent. Doing this lures the defender out of position. By twisting away from the defender at the last possible moment, the player also protects his stick from a possible check.

Bull dodge—A straight-up power dodge, executed by lowering the shoulder and barreling through the defender while power-cradling the

This defender protects the ball with a face dodge, running at the defender then turning his shoulders and pulling his stick away to his opposite side as he speeds past.
Photo courtesy of Ron Dubé Design

ball. For obvious reasons, this dodge usually requires a player with a size and strength advantage over the defender.

Roll dodge—This is another very effective dodge, especially for quicker, more agile players. After encountering pressure from a defender, the running ball carrier plants his front foot and pivots toward that foot's direction, rolling his back toward the defender and protecting his crosse with his body. Midway through this move, the player switches stick hands while the defender's vision is blocked.

A roll dodge is an effective offensive maneuver when a ball carrier and defender are running toward each other. A moment before they impact, the ball carrier plants one foot (above left) and pivots around it, rolling his back to the defender (above) and protecting his stick with his body (advanced players at this point will switch stick hands to position the ball farther from the defender). If performed correctly, the momentum of both players carry them past each other (left), which gives a big advantage to the ball carrier now moving quickly away from the defender.
Photos courtesy of Ron Dubé Design

Split dodge—Similar to the face dodge, here an exaggerated move is used to fool the defender, but instead of baiting with the stick, the ball carrier baits with body movement. Before executing this move, the player needs to decide which way he wants to come off the dodge. If he wants to go left, the stick should be in his right hand to start.

The ball carrier first takes a few steps back to establish some running room then heads full speed at his opponent, causing the defender to backpedal. At about five feet from the defender, the ball carrier begins his fake with an exaggerated step with the right foot in that direction. Once the defender takes a drop step with his left foot and twists his hips, the ball carrier plants hard on the right foot and pushes out toward the left foot, shifting his body weight and momentum to the left. While pushing off with the right foot, he then transfers the stick across his chest to his left hand and accelerates past the defenseman on the left side.

When running with the ball, players should be aware of pursuing opponents and keep their stick in front of their body. A trailing stick is an easy target.
Photo courtesy of Dave Adams Photos

Shooting Skills

Although this critical skill can always be improved, it is often ignored during practice because it is so elementary. Intense, single-minded repetition is required, and a typical team workout where the coach is running offense and defense drills for twenty or thirty players just doesn't allow that kind of individual focus. But players must practice shooting if they want to become better scorers—it's that simple—and this usually means working on their technique outside team practices.

Fortunately, shooting is something players can work on solo. The first requirement is a bag full of lacrosse balls. The object of this practice is to work on shooting, not running after balls, so a dozen or two balls are helpful. And only lacrosse balls will do—players should not use substitutes like tennis or field hockey balls because the weight and feel of the ball in the pocket is quite different, and this can affect the mechanics of cradling, throwing, and release, even to the point where it throws

THINK OFFENSE

- When passing or catching the ball, move your feet. A stationary player is a target, and a lazy player is less focused.

- Remember that the ball can move faster than a player can. Make up distances with passing.

- When catching the ball, square your body to the goal, or catch the ball with your body in position for your next move.

- After you pass a ball and the defense starts to shift, make a cut while your defender is adjusting to his new defensive position.

- If you are double-teamed or pressured by a defender, curl away from the goal to where the pressure is less. Once free, move the ball or attempt to take the defender again.

- Don't allow defenses to reset if they are sliding or in disarray. Push the ball toward the cage and exploit their weakness before they can recover.

- Make your defender work to play you—cut, sprint, pick, and constantly move, especially if playing the crease attack position. Defensemen love players who do nothing but stand still.

- While running plays or setting picks, sprint through your motions, don't walk. Avoid telegraphing your moves.

- Do not set a pick for a teammate with the ball. This only draws another defender in for a double-team.

- If your defender turns his back to you, "backdoor" this player (run out of his line of vision) or cut toward the goal. Also, if possible, cut so your man must take his eyes off the ball.

- Avoid feeding the ball from the top of the box (near the restraining line) to the crease attackman. This player has his back to the goal, and will not have

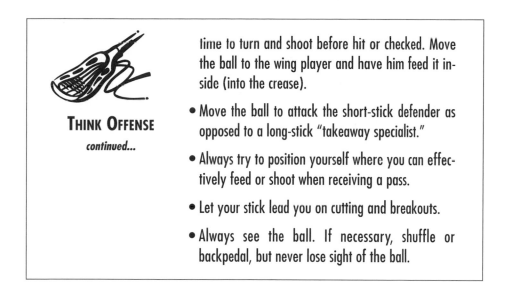

THINK OFFENSE

continued...

time to turn and shoot before hit or checked. Move the ball to the wing player and have him feed it inside (into the crease).

- Move the ball to attack the short-stick defender as opposed to a long-stick "takeaway specialist."

- Always try to position yourself where you can effectively feed or shoot when receiving a pass.

- Let your stick lead you on cutting and breakouts.

- Always see the ball. If necessary, shuffle or backpedal, but never lose sight of the ball.

off a player's routine instead of improving it. Finally, this practice should always be carried out while wearing gloves, which better replicates a real game situation.

The next task is to find an appropriate target. A lacrosse goal isn't necessarily the best target, especially for novice or less skilled shooters. Without something behind the net to stop errant shots, players may find themselves spending more time chasing balls than shooting. If possible, erect a second, larger net behind the cage, or move the goal somewhere so there is a barrier behind it, such as a baseball backstop (there's no shortage of backstops at most parks and schools). With a backstop, you don't even need a cage—the target can be imaginary, or a sheet or taped outline of a goal can be hung against the fence.

Coaches should emphasize that players always practice shooting while moving. Most of the shots taken in a game are on the run, so they might as well get used to it. Once players get a feel for shooting, they can begin to work on their mechanics. A correct grip on the stick is primary. The bottom hand acts as a stabilizer while the top hand, placed higher up the stick, provides the aim. Similar to a golf swing, it isn't the amount of muscle mass in your arms that results in a harder shot, but the coiling of the body at the waist and the torque generated when the ball is released toward the target. Twist the hips in the direction you are shooting and pull the hands back from the target with the elbows out from the sides of the body. By bringing the hands farther back and keeping the elbows up, you can get more power in the shot. Follow through with the head of the stick while snapping the wrists toward the target. The feet work in unison with the arms. Your windup begins with the back foot and the back leg redistributing your weight on the follow-through toward your front foot as you let it rip.

Be canny when shooting. Keep your intentions hidden until you take your shot, and instead of just winging it toward the goal as hard as possible, pick a location and aim. Remember that your shot doesn't need to be the fastest one you have ever taken. Placing the ball where you want it to go and where the goaltender isn't will result in more goals than blasting away. One example is shooting on the goalie's off-stick side. A goalie is weakest on this side because he needs to bring the head of his stick across his body to make the save. The area around the hip on the off-stick side is even more difficult to defend. Another good tip is to look at a spot behind the goalie when shooting and shoot with a quick release, not allowing the goalie to read and set up for your shot.

When shooting in the crease area, control and accuracy are more important than speed and power. Keep the hands about a foot apart, but choke up on the stick about ten inches from the butt end for extra control. Ultimately, a lacrosse player has a variety of shots available to him, and the best way to keep a goaltender guessing is to vary the shots you take. Be unpredictable by using a mix of the shots listed below.

Overhand shot—The most accurate and basic shot in lacrosse. This shot is difficult for goalies to read as the shooter can adjust his angle at the moment of release to aim anywhere on the net. An overhand shot is the best option when shooting on the run because of its accuracy and quick release.

An overhand shot is the most basic shot in lacrosse, offering a quick release and pinpoint accuracy.
Photo courtesy of Dave Adams Photos

Sidearm shot—Less precise than the overhand shot, the *sidewinder* offers greater velocity and power while still being fairly accurate, making it a good shot to take from the outside or when coming off a pick.

The sidearm shot creates power and velocity and can be used to shoot around defenders.
Photo courtesy of Dave Adams Photos

Underhand shot—Underhand or *submarine* shots are less accurate and consequently less often used, but they can be employed to devastating effect. The stick and ball movement from low to high is difficult for goalies to judge and can catch them off guard. A player has the option of shooting either a low, bouncing screamer, or a low-to-high rising shot toward the top corners of the cage, forcing a goalie to guess whether to cover high or low.

Underhand shots are difficult for goalies to gauge on any type of playing surface, but on turf or natural grass they will skip and bounce erratically, making these "wormburners" especially tough to stop.
Photo courtesy of Dave Adams Photos

Behind-the-back shot—This is a difficult play for beginners, and although considered a showboating shot, it does have its purpose. It can be used when a player cuts in front of the cage and draws the goalie out of position. Once the goalie makes his move, he leaves the far side of the cage open, offering the shooter a perfect opportunity to whip the ball over his shoulder or around his back and into the net.

Bounce shot—Balls often take strange hops and are difficult to judge, especially on grass or wet surfaces. This uncertainty can be played to your advantage. When executing a bounce shot, don't shoot at the goalie's feet—the ball won't have a chance to rebound before he can block it. Instead, bounce the ball near the top of the crease; that way, the shot is too far away for the goalie to stop unless he comes out of the cage, and he is forced to play the rebound.

Quick stick—A term used for catching and shooting without cradling the ball. This is done by choking up on the stick, recoiling slightly as you catch the ball, and firing—all in one smooth motion. It is an essential skill for attackmen in close (within ten yards of the goal) who are receiving passes from behind the cage.

Crank shot—When shooting from the outside, this wind-up, powerhouse shot delivers speed and power, but it requires time to get off and is generally not very accurate. The ball may be fired into the air or along the ground. Bouncing crank shots are highly unpredictable, and even more so if the field is wet. Because of their inaccuracy, crank shots should only be taken if a teammate is backing up the cage.

Sweep shot—This overhand shot is effective when moving across-field in front of the cage, decreasing the shooting angle. The shot must be made before the shooter runs out of position. The farther he sweeps, the less goal area he will have to shoot at.

Fake—A play made when an attackman is in close and attempting to draw a goalie's stick away from the intended shot. Generally, the shooter is one-on-one with the goalie. Always shoot opposite the fake—don't fake high and then shoot high, as it defeats the purpose of moving the goalie into that position. Fake high, then shoot low, or vice versa.

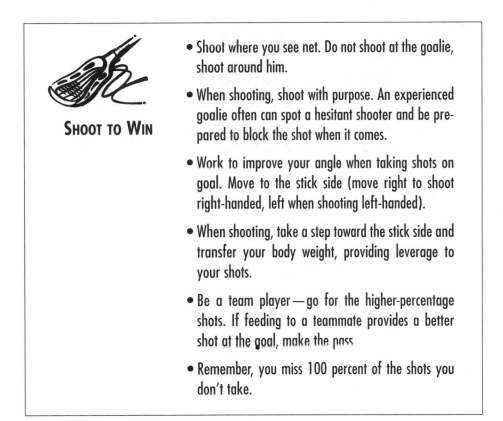

SHOOT TO WIN

- Shoot where you see net. Do not shoot at the goalie, shoot around him.

- When shooting, shoot with purpose. An experienced goalie often can spot a hesitant shooter and be prepared to block the shot when it comes.

- Work to improve your angle when taking shots on goal. Move to the stick side (move right to shoot right-handed, left when shooting left-handed).

- When shooting, take a step toward the stick side and transfer your body weight, providing leverage to your shots.

- Be a team player—go for the higher-percentage shots. If feeding to a teammate provides a better shot at the goal, make the pass

- Remember, you miss 100 percent of the shots you don't take.

Defensive Moves

To the novice or anyone unfamiliar with the sport, lacrosse can give the impression of being a violent game, with players engaging in full running contact, wielding long metal poles used to spear and beat one another. The truth is far from it, however. Lacrosse is truly a sport of speed and finesse. The playing action looks—and could be—dangerous, but body armor adequately protects the players and strict guidelines on the use of sticks are rigidly enforced.

Illegal use of the crosse draws a one-minute personal foul penalty, usually for slashing, tripping, or cross-checking. Slashing is the act of striking a player's body with a stick while attempting to dislodge the ball, unless the player is using part of his body (below his head or neck) to protect his stick. If your stick strikes any part of an opposing player's head, back, shoulders, or groin—except while you are attempting to pass, shoot, or scoop the ball—a slash is called. Any stick check that is thrown where the stick is deemed "out of control" or being swung with

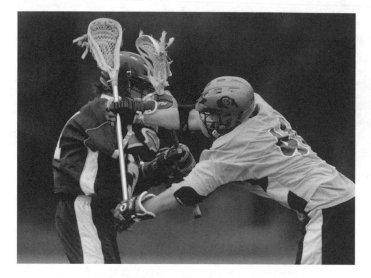

Pushing or hitting an opponent with the stick shaft as shown here is an illegal crosscheck. To avoid being flagged, a player must keep both gloves together on the shaft when making contact with an opponent.
Photo courtesy of Dave Adams Photos

malice, even if it doesn't touch the player, results in a slashing penalty. And using the crosse to trip a player earns a tripping penalty.

Body checks are illegal when directed below the waist, above the neck, or from the rear. A player who is not on his feet may not be body-checked. Hitting a player who has already passed or thrown the ball will result in a penalty if the check could have been avoided. When a body check is delivered by pushing or hitting with the crosse, a cross-check penalty is called. Using your head to butt or "spear" an opponent will result in a one- to three-minute personal foul, depending on how violent the action is. Any player who accumulates five personal fouls in a game is automatically ejected.

Sometimes penalties are avoided if the referees determine that the offense is unintentional. When a player contacts an opponent with his stick, but it is not regarded as an attempt to strike that opponent, it is

A player chasing a ground ball may not be pushed by an opponent. Often, a savvy player will fall forward if any pressure is applied to his back, resulting in a penalty for his overzealous pursuer.
Photo courtesy of Dave Adams Photos

considered a "brush" and no foul is called. In much the same way, a stick check that strikes an opponent's stick and is deflected into the player's body is often considered a brush as well.

Poke check—This simple and effective defensive check uses the full length of the defenseman's longer pole, and it can be employed even when there is some distance between the defender and opponent. Basically a spearing motion, it uses the head of the stick to push, lift, or dislodge the crosse from the opponent's hands. It is an easy check to throw while running, allowing the defender to maintain stride without overextending himself. It is not likely to draw a penalty if used properly.

Well-placed poke checks enable a long-stick defender to harass or control an opponent while maintaining his own defensive position.
Photo courtesy of Dave Adams Photos

Players should be coached to avoid swinging too hard when throwing a slap check. Referees view this as out-of-control play, which usually draws a penalty.
Photo courtesy of Ron Dubé Design

Slap check—This check uses a swinging or slapping motion of the crosse against the opponent's hands and arms or stick. It is often used in close contact with an offensive player, or when an opponent is attempting to pick up a loose ball. A defender needs to be careful, however—an overly hard or uncontrollable "baseball bat" swing will draw a penalty. Any stick contact with body parts other than the opponent's arms or head also earns a penalty.

Lift check—This is one of the most underused but effective checks a player can throw. It can be used by any defender regardless of his size, speed, or athleticism, and it works against every opponent, regardless of *his* size, speed, or athleticism. This check works just as its name implies—a player gets his stick underneath an opponent's hands and lifts their gloves or elbows straight up, rendering them unable to make a shot or pass.

A lift check, in which constant upward pressure is applied to an opponent's gloves, arms, or stick, is very effective because it disrupts the player's ability to pass and catch.
Photo courtesy of Dave Adams Photos

Wrap check—Used by short-stick defenders, this is a one-handed check against an offensive player who has his back to the defender. It is done by squaring up—positioning yourself directly behind the opponent—and "wrapping" your crosse and arm around the offensive player in an attempt to hit his stick. The defender must be careful not to maintain the wrapped position or he will be called for holding. A holding call will also be drawn if the defender uses his free hand against the offensive player's body.

Over-the-head check—This is an "all-or-nothing" check used by long-pole defensemen. When it works, the ball and sometimes even the offensive player's stick are knocked to the ground. When it misses, the defender usually finds himself out of position and the remaining defense

Wrap checks are effective for stealing a ball or disrupting an offensive play. The first photo shows an illegal wrap check as the defender comes over the top of an opponent, pushing down on his shoulders and entangling the player's arms. This play typically draws a holding penalty. The second photo demonstrates a legal check—the defender reaches around with his stick but does not hold the ball carrier or use his free hand in any way.
Photos courtesy of Dave Adams Photos

will be forced to cover. Height is an advantage with this check, as is a fast stick. The check is thrown when running with the offensive player, and it works best if he is using a one-handed cradle. The defender tries to time his move for the moment when the opponent's cradling motion is at the farthest point from his body; the defender then reaches up and over the offensive player's head in a sweeping motion, bringing his stick down on the other man's arm and stick. This move usually pulls the defenseman out of position, but if executed correctly it is a devastating check.

Kayak check—Another advanced check using a long pole, this one usually doesn't pull a defender out of position, but because of the mechanics involved it may close the distance between the defender and the

This check uses the butt end of the long stick instead of the stick head. It often takes an opponent by surprise and can be a devastating move if employed properly.
Photo courtesy of Dave Adams Photos

offensive player. The defender holds the crosse as if for a poke check, then quickly slides his bottom hand forward and snaps the butt end upward toward the opponent. This motion swings the stick up like a pendulum, lifting the opponent's stick and dislodging the ball.

Ding-dong check—A solid takeaway check using a long pole, this one tricks an opponent into moving his stick into checking position through a series of setup feints. When an opponent is cradling with one hand, the defender runs with him and attempts to hit the cradled stick over the opponent's shoulder and head (being careful not to strike the player's body). This is done two or three times until the offensive player moves his stick closer to his front side to protect it, believing the defender is trying to get at it from behind. Once the man takes the bait, the defender reaches up again with his stick but only halfway, then quickly reverses and brings his stick down on the opponent's front side where he is now carrying his stick.

Ice pick check—A one-handed short-stick check, the ice pick is done while trailing a player at full speed, using the butt end of the stick to poke at the other player's stick. This is a dangerous check to attempt, as it can easily be construed as illegal, and is only advised for more advanced players.

Checking Strategies

Once players have the knowledge of what checks are out there, coaches should instruct them on the best time to employ these checks. Too often, young players are taught to immediately check a player with the ball, regardless of the ballhandler's position on the field or the threat he is to score. One reason for this is the notion that by relentlessly hounding an opponent with checks, he will panic or make a bad pass as a result of the pressure. Another reason is that younger players just learning to use a long stick may be hesitant to attack an offensive player who is used to using a short pole, for fear of being beaten. An additional coaching gaffe is the reliance on switching hands defensively or playing what is called *cross-handed defense*, depending on what side of the field a defender is on. And while these ideas seem sound on the surface, they instill bad habits on defensemen at a young age.

In reality, depending on the defensive situation the player finds himself in, either a stick check or a focus on body positioning will be necessary.

After delivering a check, a defenseman must be careful not to entangle the opposing player or drag him down to the ground. This is considered holding, and if the opponent is carrying the ball it will result in penalty time.
Photo courtesy of Dave Adams Photos

In a situation where an offensive player is driving toward the goal, the defender should first determine his position in relation to the cage, and where he wants to direct his opponent. With an opponent charging, landing an effective slap check or a poke check would be nearly impossible and will either pull the defender out of position, or worse, result in a flag. With an offensive player attacking the cage, the lift check against the opponent's hands or arms is the safest and most effective, disrupting the dodge or shot without ever losing body position.

Defenders should always try to keep their stick out in front of an opposing player, ready to deliver poke checks, and use the length of the long shaft to their advantage.
Photo courtesy of Dave Adams Photos

The best time for a defender to throw checks is when the ball carrier is moving away from the goal. At this point, they are the least dangerous and on the defensive. The defender should be on guard though, as the offensive player may be attempting to draw his man to the outside where he can exploit footwork and positioning, and an increased distance for the first defensive slide.

In a proper defensive stance, the player's feet are square with his shoulders, knees are slightly bent, and the stick is held forward.
Photo courtesy of Ron Dubé Design

As for "cross-handed defense," there is more to debate than when to throw stick checks. Some coaches believe switching hands, or holding the stick in a right-handed position when guarding the right of the crease or in a left-handed position when guarding the left of the crease, and forming an L between the stick and frontmost elbow is the best defensive position a player can maintain. And while this L enables the defender to push the offensive player down and to the outside by trapping him between body and stick, switching hands just takes too long. With the increasing speed and quickness of offensive players, the benefit in switching hands doesn't outweigh the potential of being caught in a dodge. In addition, defensemen should be more concerned with their

Double-teaming is most effective when the second defender (shown here at left) approaches from the ball carrier's blindside, taking him by surprise.
Photo courtesy of Dave Adams Photos

footwork and in gaining leverage and power from their legs than they should be with their arms and sticks.

For the record, although we have described a number of advanced checks in this book, as a writer I would be remiss if I didn't say that some of the greatest defenders in the sport only rely on two or three checks. The poke, the lift, and the slap are the most basic and effective stick checks. Truly outstanding defensemen understand that fundamentals in body positioning and proper footwork, not fancy checks, are the keys to successful defense.

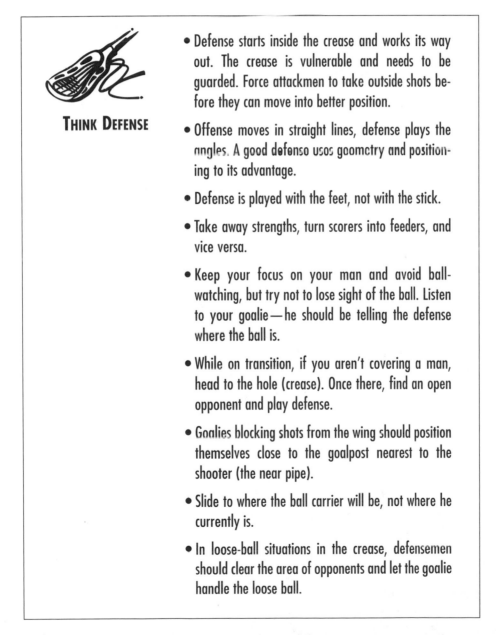

THINK DEFENSE

- Defense starts inside the crease and works its way out. The crease is vulnerable and needs to be guarded. Force attackmen to take outside shots before they can move into better position.

- Offense moves in straight lines, defense plays the angles. A good defense uses geometry and positioning to its advantage.

- Defense is played with the feet, not with the stick.

- Take away strengths, turn scorers into feeders, and vice versa.

- Keep your focus on your man and avoid ball-watching, but try not to lose sight of the ball. Listen to your goalie—he should be telling the defense where the ball is.

- While on transition, if you aren't covering a man, head to the hole (crease). Once there, find an open opponent and play defense.

- Goalies blocking shots from the wing should position themselves close to the goalpost nearest to the shooter (the near pipe).

- Slide to where the ball carrier will be, not where he currently is.

- In loose-ball situations in the crease, defensemen should clear the area of opponents and let the goalie handle the loose ball.

THINK DEFENSE

continued...

- When playing midfield defense, force your man down the side of the goal.

- When sliding, meet your player with a poke check to the hands and arms.

- Never double-team a player to his face. Your opponent will immediately spot an open teammate and pass to him.

- Prevent offensive players from receiving the ball where they can assist or score immediately. Take away the reception by checking all passes and catches.

- As the slide or double-team, you must never allow yourself to be beaten by your opponent. Finish what you start.

- Communicate, communicate, communicate! Defensive players should never be silent on the field.

Goaltending

Goaltending is probably the most visible position in the game of lacrosse, and the goalie can be the make-or-break player who determines the success of the team. No matter how good a defense you put together or how many goals your offense can score, if you don't have a goalie who can stop shots from twenty yards out, you won't win many games. Most squads have two to three goalies, with any more being difficult to manage for a coach. At least two on the roster are necessary, in case the starting goaltender draws a penalty, becomes injured, or just needs replacing after a poor outing. Some coaches play two goalies a game, with each goaltender splitting halves. This might be the case if the team has two very strong goaltenders and the coach doesn't want to favor one over the other, instead offering playing time to both. Another reason is the goalies may have different styles and the coach wants to confuse or throw off the opponent's offense, inserting a new goaltender at halftime who may be a strong finisher down the stretch. If a team has more than three goalies though, it will be difficult for the coach to find time for them all. In this case, you may want to consider suggesting that your weakest goaltender move to another position in order to get more playing time.

As a youth coach developing a team, finding a goaltender in your group is an important task. But what makes a good goaltender? First, get rid of the notion that you can take the worst stickhandler on the team and place him between the pipes. The fact is goalies need to have the best stickhandling skills on the team. Reaction time and ball handling are two of the factors that make a good lacrosse player, and goalies need those skills in spades, especially since they are burdened with a larger, less maneuverable stick. A certain sense of fearlessness and sacrifice is also required, as goalie can be a thankless job in lacrosse. Not only is it physically demanding on the body to stop shots, but you get shouldered with a lot of the blame when you lose and none of the glory reserved for the scorers when you win. Basically, being a goalie means being a leader, not only in the sense that the goalie is the leader of the defense, vocally shouting ball position and defensive sets, but also being a leader in the sense that he is prepared to do whatever it takes for his team to win, even if it means counting bruises instead of goals and assists.

Goaltending is one position in lacrosse where it is most important to develop the proper fundamentals at an early age. Once established, bad goaltending habits can be extremely difficult to break. Making changes to an established technique can be difficult and require concentration, causing a goalie's game to suffer until the new technique is absorbed. When goalies do not adhere to the basic fundamentals, however, they will struggle, and no amount of skill and talent will be able to save them.

Before we touch on the physical steps that will serve as the base fundamentals for successful goaltenders, let's address the mental preparation. Three mental aspects of goaltending you can teach that are required for success at all levels are preparedness, toughness, and aggressiveness.

Preparedness is more than just going into the game believing in a win. It means the goalie understands the way his teammates and opponents play. The goaltender is not only responsible for tracking the ball for the defense and verbally relaying its location, but also telling the defense when to slide, or what defensive set they should be in. The defense exists as a tool for the goaltender to protect the goal and prevent inside shots with a high probability of scoring. By understanding the strengths and weaknesses of his teammates, the goalie can better dictate to them how to play defense. By knowing and observing his opponent, the goaltender can learn which players are scoring threats and what types of shots they are partial to, or spot vulnerabilities in the way they carry their stick. By cataloging these observations, the goaltender will better his game.

Toughness is more than being able to take the pain of a hard rubber ball rebounding off the thigh. Toughness is being able to shake off a goal scored against you. It is about keeping a cool head while in the net, no matter what the situation. Lacrosse is a very high-scoring game and goals will be scored, even the bad ones. Demonstrate to your goalie he needs to have the courage to remain positive and focused, thinking about the next shot, not the last one. Don't let him get down on himself; there are too may people counting on the goalie and there will be plenty of time to reflect when the game is over. Teammates and opponents can read when the keeper is mentally beaten, so teach you goalie to never let anyone see it. If he lets in a goal, get your goalie to bounce right back up and show everyone on the field nothing fazes him.

Last, teach mental aggressiveness. Make your goalie believe he can stop the shots coming at him, and tell him to always act in an aggressive, forceful manner when making a save. A goaltender who doesn't believe in his ability and thinks he will not be able to make a save will most likely try to block the ball in any way possible, instead of driving the hands and stepping, as will be discussed shortly. Also, make sure your goalie isn't afraid of the ball, ducking or shifting the body to avoid being hit. If a goaltender is afraid of the ball, he should think about playing another position. By playing afraid and submissive, your goalie will not have any success. Aggressively moving toward the ball, stepping with conviction instead of waiting for the ball to come to you, is the proper technique. A goalie playing passively and lazily will only lead to the ball in the back of the net.

Now that your goaltender has the mental preparation he needs to succeed, he must establish the proper physical form and technique and build from that. The two most important aspects of instructing the goalie are (1) the goalie stance and (2) watching the ball through the end of the shot. You will see that the different steps and rules goaltenders observe are all linked to these two principles.

Step 1: Ball Tracking

Eye on the Ball, Not the Game

It is the goaltender's first instinct to watch the play of the game in front of him, how his defense is sliding, the cutting of his opponent, and the moves of the shooters. These are all distracting him and removing his focus from the ball itself. If the goaltender is not attentive and watching the ball all the time, he cannot react to it and will be unable to make a stop. If the keeper loses sight of the ball, teach him to remain calm and wait, scanning for the ball until it comes back into view and then responding. Although it only takes a fraction of a second to find the ball again, that is enough time for a quick shot or feed, so the goaltender should attempt to never lose sight of the ball.

Using the Top Hand as a Guide to Track the Ball

Using the top hand holding the stick as a visual guide is a very useful technique for goalies that allows them to follow the motion of the ball while simultaneously setting up and preparing themselves for the shot. By placing that top hand level with the eye but not obstructing it, the goaltender can point to the ball and follow it as it moves about the field, whether an opponent passes, drives, or dodges. By tracking the ball in this manner, the keeper is moving with the ball, subsequently setting up his stance behind that hand regardless of where the ball is or of its threat level at the time. By using this technique, the goalie will always be ready for the shot before it is taken and won't find himself beaten by quick stick shots off feeds to the crease or cutting players.

Don't Be Fooled by the Shooter, Maintain Fundamontals

As was already noted, concentration on the ball itself is the first and most important step to teach a developing goalie. As your goalie progresses, you may find him taking shortcuts by trying to read shooters to determine the trajectory of the ball off the shot based on their shooting motion. Reading the shooter is a useful tool, as some shooters can be predictable and a goalie can get fairly good at guessing where the ball will go. But ultimately, a guess is all it really is. An opponent with a different shot delivery or a change in an established pattern will reduce the chances of your goalie guessing correctly and usually lead to a panicked attempt to block the ball instead of making a clean save. But by maintaining that focus on the ball itself, and not being distracted by the movements of the shooter, the goalie can track the ball for longer periods of time, resulting in more clean saves.

Talk It Up

The goaltender is the general of the defense. He is the only player on the field who is supposed to ball-watch all the time and therefore is always aware of its location. Being a goalie means not being quiet and not being shy. As the balls moves positions on the field, the goaltender should be shouting with each new location, after it is passed but before it arrives at the spot, to help the defensemen know where the ball is and how to position themselves on the man they are guarding. "Top right!" "Top left!" "Bottom left!" "Ball behind!" and so on. These calls need to be forceful and clear.

In addition, the goaltender has a number of other calls that give the defense an extra set of eyes. "Check stick" should be used for any passes into the crease area, and the defensemen who hear it should immediately check the stick of the man they are guarding in an attempt to disrupt the pass. "Slide" initiates the defense rotation, and a call such as "Pick up" will tell the defender guarding the man with the ball he needs to aggressively defend since that player is getting too close to the cage. Distance calls help defenders with their backs to the goal know where they are on the field. "Twenty out" means twenty yards, and "Even" means an opponent driving from behind the net is now breaking the plane of the goal line extended and will be a step away from being in front of the net. "Clear" is the call for players to break upfield and out toward the sideline in order to move the ball outside the defensive area of the field. In addition, the goaltender can call different defensive sets based on what the team has in its playbook.

When a ball rebounds into the crease, defensive players should be ready to bodycheck any opposing players in the area, allowing the goalie to gather up the loose ball and move it away from the goal.
Photo courtesy of Dave Adams Photos

Step 2: Developing Your Goalie's Stance

Being Ready to Make the Save

Although that statement seems like a no-brainer, you would be amazed how many goalies just are not truly ready, both mentally and physically, to move to the ball and make the save. Being ready early involves not only the ball-watching techniques described above, but also assuming the proper stance.

Positioning of the Arms and Stick

By being ready early, your goalie has his hands and elbows in front of his chest, hands raised, and wrists positioned to the backside of the shaft to ensure proper stick rotation. This rotation is a propeller movement used to stop off-stick shots where the bottom hand acts as the pivot as the top hand drives toward the ball. The bottom hand must remain loose in its grip so the tighter top hand can drive freely to the ball with the range needed to reach the corners of the net. The lacrosse stick is slightly angled in the goalie's hands, with his top hand aligned with his eye without blocking his vision, and the bottom hand in front of his opposite pectoral muscle. The head of the stick should be even with the crossbar, as most shooters instinctively shoot high off feeds or when driving the net.

A player who keeps his arms close to his chest instead of out in front of him and positions his hands low instead of aligning the top hand with his eye is not ready to make a save. In this situation, by pulling the stick close to the body, the player's elbows are forced outward and the wrists now are positioned on the side of the shaft, limiting the ability to rotate the stick to make a save. Also, now when the goalie reacts, he must make longer and more time-consuming movements. By positioning the top hand in the line of vision, the goalie's hand-eye coordination improves, the speed when driving the hands and stick to the ball increases, and the body follows that hand's movement, stepping to the ball.

Positioning the Feet

The goalie's knees should be bent with his feet shoulder-width apart and his weight forward because his chest is slightly positioned out over the hips. By keeping the body's weight forward and on the balls of the feet, the goalie is ready to instinctively step quickly toward the shot. Standing on the heels will lead to a desire to backpedal and will result in a shorter, slower first step. By instructing the goalie to maintain a stance where the toes are closer in distance than the heels, the first step taken by the goalie (the ball-side foot) will result in the entire body moving toward the ball for an even faster stance.

Protect the Near Pipe

After achieving the proper stance, remind your goalie to stand slightly forward in the crease to reduce the shooter's angles, and to never be beaten pipe side. In other words, the goaltender should always position himself closer to the goalpost that is closest to the shooter, essentially "hugging" the pipe. If the ball is on the left wing, protect the left post and vice versa. This cuts off any angle the shooter has on the near pipe and forces him to take a lower-percentage shot at a more difficult angle with the goaltender standing in between. Cutting off a shot on the near pipe is crucial help for the defense when an attackman is attempting to drive the cage from behind the net or from the wing area.

Step 3: Making the Save

Driving toward the Ball

A proper stance results in the body fluidly moving toward the ball when making a save. If your goaltender has his arms positioned properly and his top hand aligned with his vision, it should feel natural to drive the top hand forward. This driving motion, coupled with the weight on the balls of the feet, leads directly to naturally stepping forward with the ball-side foot instead of side to side, attacking the shot with the body following just behind. Remind your goaltender to watch the ball from the moment it is shot until it is in the net of his stick, not altering his grip until the ball is saved.

Proactive Play versus Reactive Play

By using the techniques outlined above, including verbal cues and direction, assuming a proper stance, and driving and stepping to the ball, the goaltender is being proactive in the net and will give himself more of an opportunity to make a save than waiting for the shot and relying on reflexes alone. Coaches need to watch players in the net, making sure they are honoring the technique and not lapsing into lazy habits, which include hoping athleticism will make up for an unfocused technique.

What Next?

So the shooter has taken the shot. Now what? Well, if the shot went wide or over the top of the cage, the goalie needs to break to the end line behind the net in an attempt to beat out the opposing team and reclaim possession of the ball. Remember, the first player closest to the spot where the ball went out of bounds on the end line is the one who receives possession, not the closest player to the end line itself. If your goaltender is properly stepping for the save, he already has a jump on all other flat-footed players on the field and should continue that movement in running down the ball.

If your goaltender has made the save, but given up a rebound in front of the net, he needs to think about garnering the loose ball. Before he can be effective in doing so, he needs to know what privileges the crease provides him, and the proper action to take. As we discussed in the defensive section of this book, unless a defenseman can get a clear ground ball and move upfield, the defense should be thinking of clearing the area directly in front of the crease of offensive opponents so the goalie can clamp the loose ball. The reason is that a hastily kicked, swatted, or lobbed ball, by either team, all too often finds itself in the back of the net.

Coaches need to instruct their goalies on what they are entitled to regarding crease protection. For instance, a goaltender extended outside the crease trying to clamp a loose ball is protected from body checks if he has even one toe inside the crease, but he can still be stick checked. At this point, smart attackmen will attempt to swipe the ball from under the clamped goalie stick, which is perfectly legal, and the goaltender must work quickly to bring that ball back into the crease. Once the ball and goalie are inside the crease, any opposing player touching him or his stick in any way will draw an interference call. Once the clamped ball has been dragged back into the crease, a goaltender can take his time picking it up, with the possession count starting once he has the ball in his stick.

Once the possession count begins, the goalie has four seconds to vacate the crease or move the ball out of the crease. Your goaltender should be patient, using his time protected within the crease to look for a good passing option, and if nothing is available, exit the crease from behind the cage, looking for help from the defenders or to move the ball upfield on his own. A smart, heads-up play to teach is having your goalie draw an interference call against an attackman too close to the crease. Many times, the attackman will attempt to bat down a pass or obstruct the goaltender's vision by standing directly in front of him and the crease. If the goaltender passes the ball and the attackman touches him in any way, even if the goalie is the one initiating all movement, interference will be called and a free clear granted.

Face-Offs

Face-offs start each quarter (barring possession of the ball at the end of the previous quarter during a penalty situation) and follow every goal scored. Controlling the face-offs is a surefire way to maintain momentum—or take it away from an opponent—by gaining possession of the ball after either team scores. Face-offs are opportunities that can lead to fast breaks and quick scores. Coaches should identify midfielders who excel in this role and use them as face-off specialists. These players don't need exceptional foot speed or stick skills, only the ability to win in one-on-one face-off situations. Skills that are required are quick hands to clamp the ball, good ground-ball control, communication with the player's wingmen, and a natural ability to block and bodycheck to "box out" his opponents.

Face-offs begin when the referees call both players down into their stance. The players place their sticks firmly on the ground, parallel to the midfield line, with crosse heads matched up on edge and the ball between them (this area directly above the crosse heads and ball is considered a "neutral zone" that may not be intruded upon by either player until the whistle blows). After the referee calls "Set!" the players are not allowed to lift or move their sticks or shift position until the whistle is blown. The player who wins the contest and takes possession either moves the ball downfield or passes to another midfielder. Face-off specialists then usually exit the field in a substitution.

Many moves and countermoves regarding the face-off will be discussed; however, there are some things that will always remain consistent. The proper stance can help a midfielder's chances of winning a face-off. No two players' stances will look identical, but certain techniques should be applied. The player should line up as close to the ball as possible, every time he gets into his stance, so that he doesn't telegraph his intentions to the opponent. The player should square his hips to the opponent and lower his center of gravity, feet shoulder-width apart, weight on the balls of the feet, keeping his body to the left of his crosse. This position will provide a good center of balance and allow the player to maximize his strength. The right foot should line up with the right glove, as close to the stick head as possible, with the left foot about a foot back from the midfield line. In addition, the player's stance must allow him to keep from putting any weight on his hands. By keeping the weight off the hands, the player's quickness improves off the whistle, and in face-offs quickness is everything. A player may lean over the midline, but not over the head of his stick, keeping his head close to the ball but out of the neutral zone. The right hand also should be as close to the stick head as possible, palm facing upward, but it may not touch the plastic part of the crosse. The left hand should be positioned in the middle of the stick, about shoulder-width apart from the right hand. Keeping your hands too close together will minimize your power. Point both thumbs toward the crosse head, with the left palm facing downward. In most cases, the left hand leads, so maintain a good grip. With this hand placement, the player should be able to execute any move in his repertoire without having to change his hand placement or stance. After the whistle blows, stay as low as possible. This will keep you closer to the ball, giving you more control and allowing you to keep your stability when your opponents are pushing you around. A solid, consistent setup every time you face off, including using the same stance, hand placement, and stick head position in relation to the ball, is essential to successfully masking your planned move.

These photos show the face-off stance (top left) and the different moves a midfielder can employ to win possession of the ball. Clamping down on the ball (top right) allows the middle to redirect the ball wherever he chooses. A jump move (bottom left) prevents an opponent from clamping by blocking his stick with the head of your stick. Raking (bottom right) can lead to a fast break as the face-off midfielder takes the ball and runs.
Photos courtesy of Dave Adams Photos

The basic movement for the face-off is as follows: when the whistle is blown, the left hand twists the stick toward the ball and drives forward. The right hand remains firm. By positioning your feet correctly you increase the power of your draw. The right foot stays in its position, acting as a pivot while the player steps forward with the left foot. Once the player has control of the ball, he can draw the ball forward, between his legs or toward his goal.

Face-off midfielders will develop their own moves and tricks as they gain experience, and these moves are designed to implement a fast break. The three most common face-off techniques include the clamp, the rake, and jumping, or "topping," the ball. These moves all have their strengths, and their weaknesses. Think of "rock, paper, scissors"—in most cases, clamp beats the rake, rake beats the jump, and the jump often beats the clamp.

Clamp—This is the most popular and fundamental face-off move, in which the crosse head is flipped to face downward and used to trap the ball against the ground before the opponent can take possession. The opposing player will work hard to dislodge it, and keeping the ball immobile too long will draw a withholding call, so you must move quickly. One move is to pull the ball between your legs and send it to a wingman positioned behind you or rake it forward for yourself and a fast break.

The clamp is the best countermove for an opponent using the rake.

Rake—The rake pulls the ball out immediately without clamping it to the ground. The left hand is again thrown forward and the stick is rotated so the bottom edge of the crosse head can claw the ball toward your left side. Depending how fast and hard the ball is raked out, the midfielder can either garner the loose ball himself by stepping to the left, or push it out to a wingman.

The rake is usually the best countermove to the jump. Because topping moves come over the ball, an unsuspecting player can be fooled by an opponent who comes underneath with a quick, forward move called a *punch rake*.

Jump—Jumping or "topping" is the most difficult of the three basic face-off moves, one that requires quick hands and a bit of precision. When the whistle blows, the left hand moves forward, the stick is lifted off the ground, and, with both hands leading, the stick head is "jumped" over the ball. Then the hands quickly pull the stick back, the player plants his right foot forward and pivots, boxing out his opponent as he scoops up the ball.

Timing is crucial in face-offs, and it is important to concentrate on the whistle and anticipate when it is going to be blown. That will help you start your move and get a jump on your man. Beware that any cheating or illegal advantage will result in a loss and the ball being awarded to the other team. Some things the referees watch for include lifting the hands or moving the body before the whistle; tilting or moving the crosse head early; using the glove to play the ball; stepping on, laying the shoulder on, or holding another player's crosse; kicking the opponent's stick; violating the neutral zone; or withholding the ball from play.

During face-offs, the attack and defense remain in the restraining boxes at each end of the field until possession is called by the referees. Midfielders wait in the wing areas, usually one long-stick and one short-stick player from each team on each side of the field. The long-stick "mid" should always line up on the right of his face-off player—the defensive side of his opponent—to prevent the fast break. The short-stick man lines up on the left side of his face-off player, looking to pick up a ground ball directed to him or ready to box out his opponent.

It's a good idea for teams to go into face-offs with a strategy. These are fluid situations that often require on-the-spot adaptation, but the wingmen should at least know what their face-off man is planning before he gets into his stance. For example, it helps if the short-stick midfielder knows where his man is going to put the ball, or if the face-off man will try to take it himself and require a box-out. Both wingmen should talk to their face-off man as they run in, telling him their locations and letting him know they are available as outlets. They should also talk to one another, allowing the closer player to go for the ball while the other assumes the fast break responsibility. Wingmen also must time their moves carefully, as officials look for them to jump in before the whistle and watch for illegal body checks.

CHAPTER 5

PRACTICE/COACHING DRILLS

Line Drills

Line drills are a staple of lacrosse, used to warm up players before games and practices. For beginners, they teach the basic movements and stick skills that will carry them through their careers. For advanced players, they are an opportunity to get the sticks moving and teammates focused on the task at hand. Because line drills are simple and can run themselves, they also give coaches time to work with the goalies while the rest of the team practices.

Only half the field is required for line drills. Two groups of players face one another on each side of the field between the restraining box line and sideline, maintaining a distance of about forty yards apart. Optimally, there will be three to four players in each group, so the lines have no more than six or eight people. This allows plenty of running and practice and keeps players from waiting too long for their turn. Long poles and defensive midfielders may be grouped together in a line behind the net, while two lines of short-pole players work out above the cage. This allows the coach room to shoot to the goaltender.

One group starts with a ball and moves at a casual speed toward the other group, advancing the ball depending on the drill being performed. The player who passes moves to the end of the line, as the receiving player then advances toward the other group. Captains or coaches can change drills after each player gets a couple of repetitions.

Right-to-Right Throwing/Catching

Begin with the basics. All players start with the stick in their right hand, which for most will be their stronger hand. The players holding the balls run toward the opposite group and pass to them who catch while running, and brisk passes are made back and forth as long as possible within the drill. The focus is on moving the feet and catching in stride. Also, teams that practice communicating in drills (receivers yell "Here's your help!" to the passing player) will carry that habit onto the field and into their games.

Left-to-Left Throwing/Catching

The same as above, but now all sticks are held in the left hand, so most players will be using their weak hand. Be warned—this can be ugly with beginners! But the more use players get with their "off" hand, the greater the threat they become on the field. An ambidextrous ball carrier who can shoot accurately with either hand is difficult to defend.

Right Pass to Left Catch

This drill has the same dynamics as above, teaching players to switch hands to keep their sticks inside or outside to protect them from defenders. Two lines of players move in a clockwise circle around the crease, the outer ring making left-hand tosses to the inner players who are catching and returning the throws with sticks held in their right hands. Reverse the rotation and the opposite happens—the inner group now holds their sticks in their left hands, while the outer ring of players have them in their right. This drill also gives players practice swapping stick hands while carrying the ball. The switch should be made in one clean motion by bringing the stick head across the body with the top hand while the bottom hand releases. The bottom hand receives the stick on the other side, taking hold above the hand that brought it over.

Ground Balls To

Ground balls are a major part of lacrosse play and should be practiced often. The call "Ground Balls To" signals receiving players that the balls will be rolling and they should be ready to scoop them up. Carried out one at a time, a player starting with the ball runs halfway toward the other group, then rolls the ball toward a teammate. Receivers should practice keeping their bodies in front of the ball to block a bad hop, and lowering the butt ends of their sticks for the scoop. After each player picks up a ball and cradles it, he rolls it out for the next in line.

Ground Balls Away

Similar to the above, this drill has the added element of a pass to help roll the ball along. One player throws a long pass while running toward an intended receiver, who at this point is somewhat stationary (you should always move the feet when throwing and catching, but the receiver doesn't run just yet). As he catches the ball, the receiver immediately throws it back to the passer, who takes it on the fly and flicks the ball behind him. Now the ball is rolling away from the original receiver, who must chase it down.

Over-the-Shoulder

This breakout drill involves three players and helps sharpen team coordination. Here's how it works: Player A runs the ball across the field to the receiving group. Receiving Player B—the breaking player—then pops out of the line a few feet (the stick in his hands should point upfield, indicating the direction he will take). The player behind him in line, Receiving Player C, calls "Help!" and takes the pass from Player A. Once he has the ball, Receiving Player C yells "Break!" releasing Receiving Player B to run upfield. Player C then throws and Player B catches the ball over his shoulder on the run.

Passing Drills

Monkey in the Middle

A center player is situated between two outside players. The left player throws the ball to the center player, who then throws the ball back to the left player. The center player then turns to face the right player. The right player throws the ball to the center player, who then throws the ball back to the right player. The center player turns to face the left player and the drill starts again.

Pinwheel Passing

This remedial drill for youth players focuses on maintaining eye contact, communication, passing accuracy, and release quickness. Four outside players rotate about twenty to thirty feet away from four stationary center players. The center players throw the ball to the outside players, who then throw the ball back to the center players, rotating and repeating. As players develop a feel for the drill, make modifications such as all left hands or quick sticks.

Down the Line

In this fast-paced drill six players stand across from one another three players wide. The players maintain a repetitive catching and throwing motion between two players. Four balls are kept in motion in order from Players 1 to 2, 2 to 3, 3 to 4, 4 to 5, 5 to 6, and completed with Player 6 throwing across (above) the formation back to Player 1.

A	Attack
M	Midfield
D	Defense
DM	Defensive Midfield
G	Goaltender
P	Player
- - - >	Pass
— >	Running Man
P ▶	Man with Ball
I	Set Pick
▲	Opposing Player

KEY TO PLAY DIAGRAM SYMBOLS

Four-Corner Outside Passing

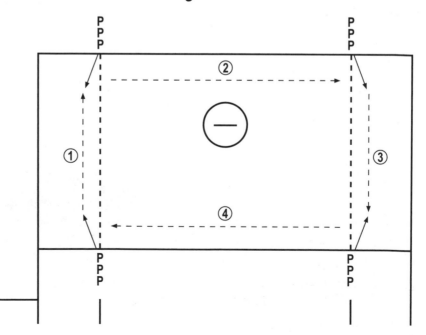

This is a simple drill for all players that can greatly increase their ability to pass and catch in game situations. Start by creating four even lines at each corner of the restraining box. In this illustration, the bottom left corner starts with the ball. He passes clockwise to the top left corner player who calls for help and makes a short break toward the passer. The player that passed the ball fills into the line he passed to, while the receiver continues moving the ball around the box. The ball is passed around this way and the sequence can be reversed after sufficient time. Extra balls can be added once players have the drill down. Intro players can use their strong hand, but more advanced players should work to keep their sticks to the outside.

Four-Corner Breakout

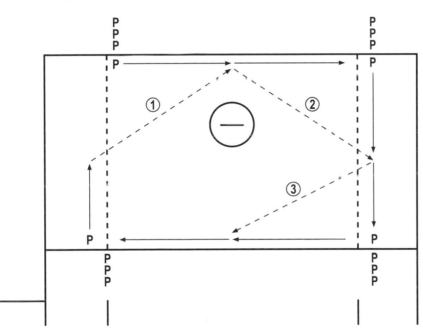

Similar to the Four-Corner Outside Passing drill, the extra wrinkle here is that the players don't move toward the passer. Instead, they break out toward the next line and catch the ball on the run. The passes travel diagonally, and shooters should lead the receivers who run at full speed.

Three-Man Passing

This full-field passing drill emphasizes passing to adjacent players while running downfield. It also reinforces changing stick hands and cross-body passing while teaching players to keep their sticks upfield and lead with their passes.

Players form three lines on an end line facing the opposite end of the field. One line stands directly in the center of the end line with the other two lines about ten to fifteen yards to the left and to the right (the sides of the restraining box). Players are instructed to keep their sticks upfield and maintain the spread distance. The rightmost line players have their sticks in their right hands, the leftmost line players have their sticks in their left hands. The center line player must switch hands depending on the player he is passing to or receiving from. The first player in each line steps forward and begins a half-speed run straight downfield toward the opposite end line, and starting with the player in the middle line, they pass the ball back and forth. Once the players are twenty yards downfield, the coach can release the next group of three players. After reaching the opposite end line, the players wait for the final group to finish and reform their lines and repeat the exercise in the opposite direction.

Three-Man Passing with Weave

This full-field passing drill emphasizes passing to crisscrossing players while running downfield. It strengthens the changing of stick hands and cross-body passing while teaching players to keep their sticks upfield and lead with their passes. Players line up in the same formation as in a regular Three-Man Passing drill. Instead of maintaining a straight line while moving downfield, players instead "weave" as they run. To do so, the center player again starts with the ball and begins to run straight downfield. He motions a pass to the line on his right. At this point, the player on the right breaks diagonally toward the center of the field, staying ahead of the player in the middle line. The middle line player passes to the player from the line on the right, and then breaks to the right side of the field, taking that player's place. Now, the rightmost player has become the middle line player and motions a pass to the leftmost line. The player in the leftmost line breaks diagonally toward the center of the field, staying ahead of the middle line player. The middle line player passes to the player from the leftmost line and then breaks to the left side of the field, taking that player's place. This weave continues until the three players reach the opposite end line.

Two Men in the Middle

A quick, small-group passing drill, this one emphasizes rolling off picks. Players assemble into groups of four players each, forming a twenty-yard line with one player on each end and two players back-to-back in the middle. The players on the end of the line each start with a ball and face the players in the middle. At the whistle, the interior players roll off one another and catch a pass from the players on the outside. After receiving the pass, the players roll off again and reverse direction, passing the ball back to the outside player on the opposite side of the line.

Four Corners and Two Balls

A good drill for beginners, this quick ball movement practice hones reflexes. Four players form a square with two opposite players each holding balls. Players pass the balls around the square without letting the second ball catch up to the first. Begin by passing clockwise, moving to counterclockwise, diagonal, and then freestyle.

Star (Five Point Passing)

A variation on line drills, this multifeatured practice incorporates almost all of lacrosse's skills in a fastpaced exercise. Players form lines at each point of a five-pointed star. The player who begins the drill passes from his line to an opposite point on the star, joining the end of the line he passed to. The player who received the ball passes to an opposite point, but not the line he received the ball from, joining the line he passed to, and so on. Names need to be used when passing to increase team communication. All passes and catches need to be in the invisible box surrounding the head and shoulders where the stick should be the target. A bad pass or catch will result in a five-push-up or sit-up penalty.

Once every player has had two turns with basic passing, change the exercise to include off-hand passing and catching, cross-handed passing, ground balls, players executing dodges after receiving a pass, and even more elaborate variations such as rolling in a particular direction, split dodging, and finishing with a behind-the-back pass. This drill is only limited by imagination.

Three-Man-Two-Ball

This passing drill can be done with small groups of players. Players work on rolling away from pressure after receiving the pass. To start, three players form a triangle with one player holding the ball. Player 1 passes to Player 2 who catches, pivots, rolls, and passes back to Player 1. Player 1 then passes to Player 3 for the same execution. Passes must be quick and precise with players rolling off in tight, exact movements.

Full-Field Passing

This drill uses the entire field, and your entire team. Goalies set up in the cages at each end of the field. Between them, on each sideline, are three evenly spaced and numbered groups. The middle groups position themselves on the midfield line. Each goalie starts with a ball, and at the whistle he passes to the player from the line on his immediate right, who begins breaking toward the middle of the field. That player catches the ball on the run, then passes to an opposite midfield group player, who breaks toward the ball. The midfield player continues to move up-field, passing the ball to a player in the line upfield and opposite, who breaks in front of the goalie. The player receiving that ball then passes to the goaltender, who starts it all again by passing to the line on his right. After each pass, the passer files into the line he threw to. The goalies always stay in the cage. Once things are moving, multiple balls may be added or play can stop and the goalies can reverse the direction of the drill.

Defense Long Passes

During play, defensemen spread wide to avoid coverage when clearing the ball, so they need to be able to make accurate, effective cross-field passes that don't fly out of bounds. This drill is good practice for them. While the coach works with the offense, the defensemen set up in a box similar to the Four-Corner drills, but with players forty to fifty yards apart. Following the same drill pattern, the defensemen work on passing to a point or passing to a man on the run.

Shooting Drills

Feed and Shoot

This is a great pregame warm-up to get a team hitting the back of the net. Two lines of players face one another on each side of the cage: one line at the top of the restraining box, the other behind the goal line. With sticks to the outside, the restraining box group cuts toward the cage while the goal line group passes upfield to the cutter. This receiver takes a quick shot and both players trade lines. Nothing fancy, this drill should be rapid fire—quick-stick shots and sharp feeds (no goalies on this drill).

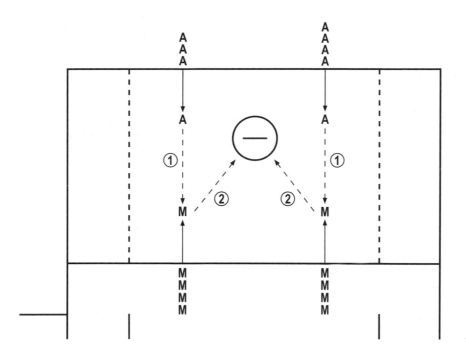

Pass, Cut, and Shoot

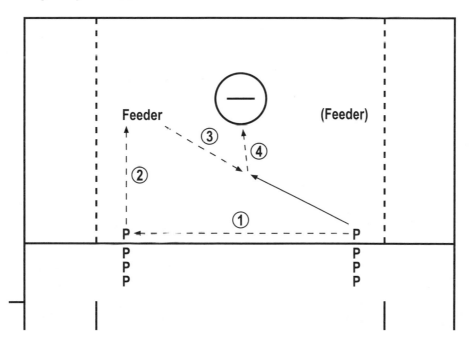

In this drill, players form up in two lines on each side of the restraining line. Two feeders are positioned at each side of the crease. The feeders do not change, so attackmen or the coaches themselves usually play those positions. The player in line on the right side of the field starts with the ball and passes to the line on the left, but doesn't yet follow or fill lines. The player who receives the ball passes downfield to the stationed feeder. As soon as the pass is thrown to the feeder, the player who began the drill cuts toward the feeder, who makes a diagonal pass to the cutter. That player catches and shoots, filling into the line opposite from where he started. A variation on this drill includes four lines, set up like the Four-Corner drills, with the two end-line groups acting as feeders and rotating after delivering the pass.

Over-and-Around Shooting

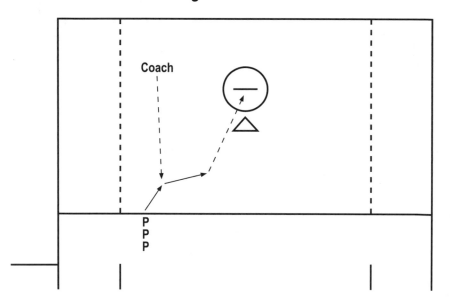

This drill is good for working on shot placement. First, position one cage directly in front of another a few yards apart (or stagger the cages). The shooting player must take a pass and then shoot over (or around) the first goal into the second. To shoot into the rear cage with another directly in front of it, the shooter almost has to hit the crossbar of the first goal to make a quality shot into the second. With staggered cages, the shooter cuts on an angle, working to increase his target visibility before release.

Off-Pick Shooting

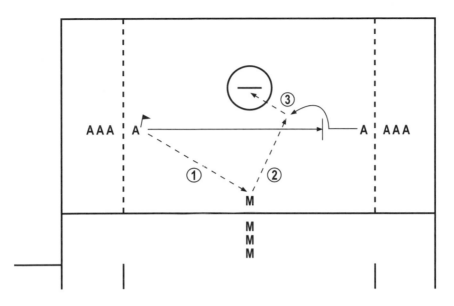

Here's a way to emphasize the pick while your team works on shooting. Position three evenly numbered groups of players, one at the top of the box and one on each sideline just above the goal. One of the attackmen starts with the ball. After a pass to the midfielder, that attackman executes a pass-and-pick-away, setting a pick for the other attackman who will come off the pick for a shot on goal. This drill can start with any player and pass to any player, as long as the pick-away rule is observed.

Long-Range Shooting

With the goal positioned in the crease, players start at the midfield line and take a running shot, releasing the ball at about thirty yards. The player then shoots a second ball from the restraining line at twenty yards, followed by another ball about ten yards out. Players should focus on shot placement. The idea with this drill is that the goals will look bigger to a player at a regular shooting distance after taking shots from so far outside.

Dodge and Re-Dodge

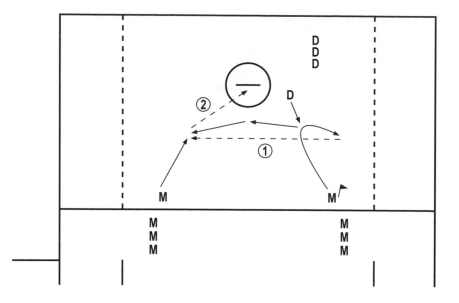

Two groups form up at the midfield line on each side of the field. One line sets up off the goal line as defenders. One of the midfield line players starts toward the goal with the ball, where he is met by one defender. The player with the ball practices rolling away from pressure, while the defender slides back into the hole. After rolling away, the midfielder passes to the second midfield line. The receiver executes one dodge and shoots. Defenders play light defense in this drill—no stick checks—and act more as a catalyst for the drill than someone aggressively trying to take the ball.

Face-Off Drills

Face-off skills improve through repetition. Here are some basic face-off drills that can help improve midfield specialists.

Move/Countermove

Coach acts as the referee, setting up a face-off between two face-off specialists. Player A is instructed to use the clamp for the first ten face-offs while Player B is instructed to use the jump counter against him. Rotate the sequence till both players have done ten clamps, jumps, and rakes. Coaches should identify problems with each player's technique and setup, instructing the player on improvements he can make.

Beat the Whistle

Repetition is the only way to hone your body and ear to increase your quickness off the whistle. In this drill, players go through the setup and starting routine over and over, trying to time their jump and anticipate the whistle without a false start. It may be difficult in the beginning, but it is something a player can improve.

Center of Gravity

The face-off man maintains a low-centered face-off stance while the coach tosses balls at him. He then picks them up as quickly as possible while keeping his center of gravity low the entire time.

Butt-End Face-Off

Two players assume the face-off position but reverse their sticks so that the stick butt ends match up, with or without a ball between them. At the whistle, the players challenge each other as if they are fighting over a ball, but the object of this drill is to work on hand speed and body position instead of focusing on the ball.

Ball Drop

Dropping a ball into a practice face-off, hockey style, instead of placing it on the line, allows face-off specialists and wingmen to work on ground balls and body position.

One-on-One Face-Off

This face-off is repeated in rapid-fire fashion, and the focus is on clamping and drawing out the ball. As soon as the ball is clamped, the whistle blows and the practice begins again.

Ground Ball Box-Out

This drill concentrates primarily on the wingmen. Two wingmen work together against a face-off player. One wing boxes out the player while the other goes after the ball.

Three-on-Three Short-Field

Two players face off with two wingmen on each side. The face-off winners get the ball and go on the offensive, trying to break past the defense. The defense players practice stopping the fast break.

Goalie Drills

These specialty drills and exercises are designed to help goaltenders with decision making and footwork. Coaches can work with the goalies while players run other drills.

When first taking shots on the goalie, start by taking half-speed shots in a progression from one side of the cage to the other, moving the feet when shooting. For example, move in a crescent motion from the left side of the field to the right side standing about ten to fifteen yards out from the cage, shooting only high shots. When reaching the right side, begin working your way back, taking midlevel shots, and finally, bounce shots. After this progression, increase the shot speed, working toward 100 percent and shooting on all areas in a freestyle scenario. Be sure to communicate to the goalie so he is prepared for the types of shots you will be taking, and avoid a close point-blank blast, as an injury may occur. While shooting, watch the goalie's form and steps, ensuring he is properly tracking the ball and driving through on the save.

Shooting Arc

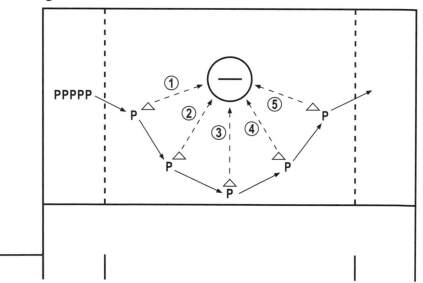

An arc of five cones is placed fifteen yards in front of the net. A shooter stands at each cone, with a line to fill the shooting positions off the sideline. Each player takes a shot in succession at the goalie, then moves to the next cone. Not all goalies like to perform this drill with the hard lacrosse balls, so check with the goalie before subjecting him to the barrage (rubber balls may be substituted). This drill helps goalies develop positioning and ball tracking as they cover each angle, while shooters work to pick their shots and shoot around the goalie.

Goalie on a String

This is a common way to teach young goalies crease positioning. By threading two ropes between the cage crossbars and holding the ends of the ropes at shooting distance, the coach creates a narrow, triangular corridor for the goalie to stand inside. The lesson here is that wherever the coach moves on the shooting arc, the goalie will be in position as long as he is centered in the triangle.

"Fungo" Stick Drills

By shooting tennis balls at your goalies, you can take a lot of practice shots without wear and tear on your men. The lightweight tennis balls also let goalies learn to feel the ball and give with the shot. To make things more challenging for the goalie, variations on this drill can be used.

Heavy bar—Give goalies an iron bar or heavy wood pole instead of a crosse. An aluminum crosse shaft filled with sand also works well. The idea is similar to baseball players using weighted "fungo" bats to warm up in the on-deck circle. The weight slows the stick speed considerably, but when the goalie switches to his regular stick it will feel light and his speed will increase.

Attack stick—The second option is to give the goalie a short attack stick to defend his goal. With its shorter length and smaller head opening, this stick is more of a challenge when it comes to stopping shots in the heart of the pocket.

Shaft only—Last, have the goalie turn his stick upside down and use only the shaft to swat at the shots. At first, the goalie just tries to make contact, deflecting the balls as they fly at the goal. As he gets better at it, he will be able to hit the balls solidly and redirect them back at the shooter.

Goalie Calls the Shots

This is an excellent thirty second exercise with two groups of players competing. A goalie starts with the ball and four long-stick players are arranged in a box on the field around him. The goalie passes to one of the defenders and, while the ball is in flight, calls out which player the receiver passes to next. The goalie continues to call out the direction of the ball, and the defense tries to complete as many passes as possible in the allotted time. When their thirty seconds is up, a second group of defensemen tries to beat the previous team's score. This drill teaches goalies to be leaders of the defense, emphasizes their communication skills, and establishes them as field leader.

Team Drills

4-on-3 Slide

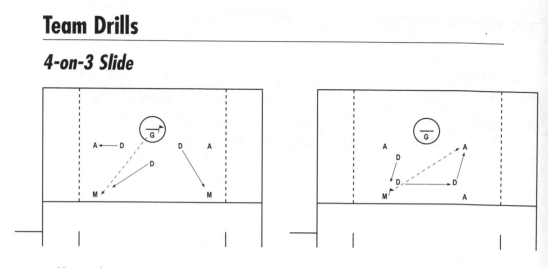

Offense forms a box, with three defenders and a goalie playing within. The goalie starts with the ball, passing it to an offense player and causing the defense to react. Using the rules of 4-on-3 transition play, the defense slides to the ball (see the "Slides" section in chapter 6) as it moves around the box, while the offense tries to find the open man for the shot. A great pregame warm-up, this drill gets the defense talking and sliding, while offense gets practice moving the ball.

4-on-4 Pressure

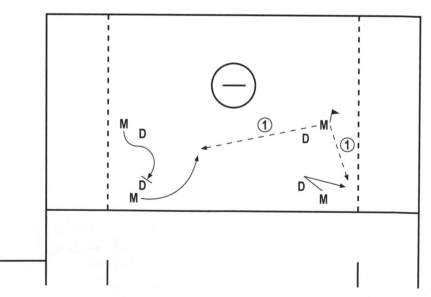

Offense forms a box, with four defenders covering the players. The offense must make four passes in a row against an aggressive defense without allowing the ball to hit the ground. Players can use V-cuts, picks, and rolling away from pressure to get open.

Half-Field Reaction

In this drill, all of the offense and one coach are positioned behind the restraining line. Off the field on one sideline are the defensemen and another coach. The offensive coach sends out any number of players with the ball. The defensive coach reacts, but sends one player less. The defense adapts to the situation and works to stop the ball. As the drill continues, the defense coach can mix it up, sending one more and creating a double-team opportunity.

Numbers

Age range: experienced to advanced

Purpose: spontaneous exercise in which the defense must adapt to an unsettled situation and an unknown number of offensive attackers.

Execution: one coach gathers the offensive players in the center of the midfield line and one coach gathers the defensive players on one sideline at goal line extended. The offensive coach sends out a select number of players, from two to six, and the defensive coach must respond with fewer players than the offensive coach sent out. The defense must react to the unsettled situation and the drill is played until the offensive team scores or the ball goes out of bounds. Note: this drill works best when coaches write a script beforehand, only telling their players how many of them are being sent from their side. It can be done spontaneously: the offensive coach shouts a number prior to sending out his players; the defensive coach sends out one less player.

2-on-2 Alley

This is a more advanced drill designed to let players practice advancing the ball from the face-off in the game's last two minutes, without stepping into the attack area and drawing a "keep it in" call. One player starts with the ball at the restraining box line, guarded by one defender. The ball carrier tries to evade his defender while attempting to pass to a teammate within the restraining box, who is also covered by a defender. This drill has two objectives: passing the ball within a confined area, and doing it within a limited period of time.

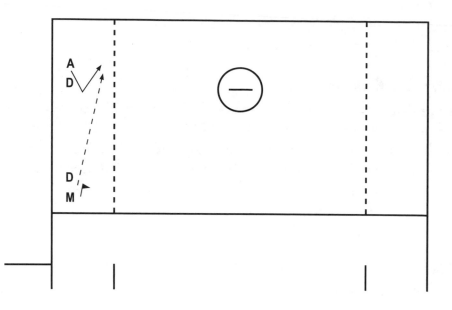

Formation Calls

The purpose of this advanced drill is for players to learn to adapt to varying field situations. The coach stands at the midfield line with the balls.

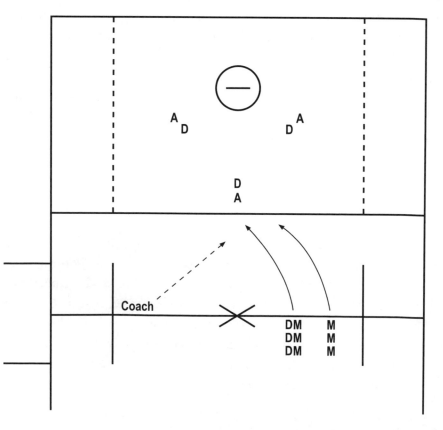

Three defensemen and three attackmen position themselves by the cage, with all remaining defense and attack players waiting off the sideline to rotate in. The midfielders form two lines at the midfield line, one line designated as offensive midfield, and the other as defensive midfield. Coach rolls out a ball and calls out a formation such as "4-on-3!" or "6-on-6!" The correct numbers of men to complete the formation are released from each line. In a 5-on-4 situation, two offensive midfielders are released, while only one defensive midfielder is released. Offense picks up the ball and play lasts until a goal is scored, the ball goes out of bounds, or the ball is cleared.

Three-Ball

This is a fun game where teams of six players compete for points. In this drill the offense has only three balls to score with. Start with the balls placed on the restraining line. As the first is picked up by the offense, the game begins. If a ball hits the ground on a dropped pass, or goes out of bounds, that ball is dead and the offense has to head back to the restraining line to grab another. This gives the offense three opportunities to score, receiving a point for each ball scored, while the defense earns a point each time the offense fails. The balls can be in play as fast as the offense can bring them out, so the defense needs to be on its toes.

East/West

Age range: experienced to advanced

Purpose: requiring only a half field and a small number of players, the team practices unsettled situations that quickly switch from 3 versus 2 from behind the cage to 4 versus 3 from the top of the restraining box. Stresses heads-up play and adjustment on the fly.

Execution: three attackmen line up on the end line behind the cage with two midfielders at the top of the restraining box. These are the offensive players. Two defensemen position themselves in the crease. When the first whistle is blown, the three attackmen attempt to score on the two defensemen from behind the cage. If they score or the ball is thrown out of bounds, a second whistle is blown stopping play. Immediately the coach calls out the name of one attackman who then joins the defensemen in playing defense, and a third whistle is blown sending the midfielders into action from up top, turning the drill into a 4 versus 3 situation. Keep switching back and forth between 3 versus 2 and 4 versus 3 while changing the attackman who assumes the defense role.

Five-Second Passing

Age range: beginner

Purpose: full- or three-quarter-field transition drill using limited numbers of players and requiring a pass every five seconds or until the ball is turned over. This prevents larger and more advanced players from running downfield every time and scoring.

Execution: with six players on each team (two attack, two midfield, two defense), begin with a face-off. The winning team must move the ball toward the goal, without any player holding the ball for longer than five seconds. If the ball is not passed within that time, the team loses the ball.

Crease Rotation

Age range: beginner to advanced

Purpose: a 6 versus 5 half-field drill that stresses the rotation and replacement of the crease player while the offense is moving the ball.

Execution: six offensive players start in a 1–3–2 set with five defenders playing a 3–2 zone. The offense moves the ball around the perimeter with the creaseman popping out to receive a pass and then having another offensive player fill in for him. The offense continues to fill and replace at the crease, while maintaining the balance of whatever set they are currently in.

Back-to-Back Cages

This is a great drill if you're limited in space. Requiring two cages and two goalies, it can be played with a small number of players and is a very intense, fun drill that allows players to work both offense and defense in a short period of time without having to stop.

Set up two goals back-to-back at the center of the midfield line with the front of the goals facing away from each another. A goalie guards the mouth of each cage. One coach stands in each crease on opposite ends of the field facing the front of the goals. Players are divided into two equal teams and the number of players depends on the scenario the coach wants. The drill can be run 2 versus 2, 3 versus 3, 4 versus 4, and so on. Each team is given a goal to defend. A face-off at the midfield line determines which team starts first. The team securing the ball becomes the offense and attacks the defensive team's goal. Play continues until there is a turnover or a goal is scored. In the case of a turnover, the defensive team becomes offense and is allowed to attack the other team's goal. Before they can take a shot, they must first pass to the coach in front of the goal they are attacking. This allows time for the other team to assume their defensive positions and prevents a one-on-none with the goalie. Play continues until a winning score is reached.

Progression

This full-field drill starts with three defenders and three attackers on each side of the field and goaltenders in each cage. Beginning as a fast break for one team, this drill ends with two full teams on the field, and very tired midfielders. With the midfield lined up on the sideline as in a game scenario, one middie steps on the field and starts a fast break. After the fast break ends, regardless of outcome, the goalie passes to his team's midfielder who is breaking out of the box. The midfielder who started the drill now becomes a defender trailing a fast break. This continues until all six midfielders have entered the game. A great conditioning drill, it involves lots of running up and down the field.

Full-Field Fast Break

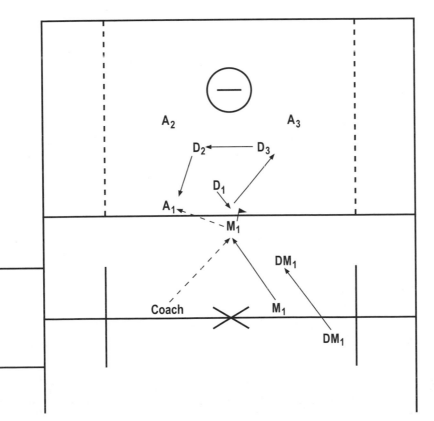

This advanced drill can be run on half the field using one cage, or full-field with both goals. The object is to practice both offensive and defensive rotations during the fast break, which occurs often in lacrosse. The dynamics of the fast break are explained in the "Transition Play" section in chapter 6—only the drill itself is described here.

To start, the coach puts three attackmen and three defensemen in position on the crease, with a goalie in the cage. The attack and defense can be arranged into set triangles when first learning this drill, so they will learn the placement and movements of each position. Once a point man is chosen for both the offense and defense, and the slide and passing rotations have been explained, the drill is ready to start. At the center line, the long- and short-stick midfielders form a line, with the player at the head of the line receiving a ball, either on a pass or a ground-ball roll. The ball carrier attempts to run through the crease for the shot. If he draws the point defenseman, he makes a pass against the defensive slide, most likely to the point attackman who will shoot or continue to pass within his triangle. A missed shot will be chased by the midfielder; if the goalie makes a save, the ball is passed back to the midfielder who then breaks upfield.

After the drill is established, the coach can add a "chaser" or trailing player. This allows the fast break to develop, and teaches the offense that they have only a short time before defensive players arrive to help, as well as teaching the defense to hurry back into the crease to find the open man. The chaser lines up five to ten feet behind the ball carrier, and goes on the same whistle that begins the drill. If the chaser can catch the ball carrier there is no fast break, and the teams play 4-on-4. Another wrinkle is that once the defense and attack understand the movements of the fast break, they should not be in their triangles at the start of the drill. They would stand closer to the restraining line, as in a game situation; when the break starts, they then fall back into the crease and into their respective positions, yelling "Fast break!" to alert one another of the situation.

Unsettled Clearing

This half-field exercise is useful for practicing clearing the ball after a shot. The coach first makes a weak shot on the goalie. The goalie pretends to make a save and yells "Clear!" The two defenders closest to the goal line extended break toward each sideline. The defensive midfielders break out at ninety-degree angles, using V-cuts to turn back toward the

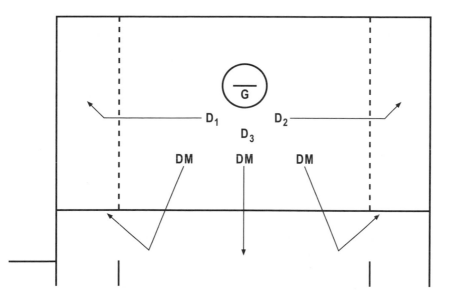

ball if covered. The remaining defenseman hangs back above the crease until the ball is moved upfield, or he can break up the sideline on the opposite (substitution) side of the field to the top of the restraining line.

A key element to this drill is the four-second rule for clearing a ball from the crease. In those four seconds, goalies are taught to take a progression of "looks" downfield to locate an open receiver before clearing the ball: the first look is toward the direction of the shot. This often provides the best opportunity for a fast break as the shooter's defender is now behind his opponent and open downfield. The goalie's second look is elsewhere downfield to find another open teammate. The third look is to the lower breaking midfielders opposite to where the shot came from. If all three looks fail to find an open receiver, in the final second the goalie runs out of the crease behind the goal, where the ball can be moved to defenders who have broken out to the wings. The goalie should avoid moving the ball up the substitution box side of the field. This area may look open, but traffic in and out of the box makes it a very dangerous area.

Ground Ball Drills

Three-Man Ground Ball

Three lines of players are evenly spaced within a few feet of each other. The first three players of each line lie on their backs, with the coach standing behind them. The coach rolls out a ball about ten yards in front of the players. On the whistle, the players jump up and attempt to retrieve the ground ball. The two players on the outside are on the same team. They attempt to work the man/ball scenario, with one man blocking the opponent, allowing his teammate to garner the loose ball. Once the ball is secured, one pass has to be made before the players can return. If the lone player in the middle gets the ground ball, he makes a pass to the coach.

Variation: three players stand behind a line and the center player throws the ball out about twenty to thirty yards. The two end players attack the ground ball while the center player sprints in a fifteen-yard V-cut to get "open" for a pass from the player who secures the ball. The player who picks up the ground ball carries it and dodges to about half the distance to the starting line, feeding the ball to the center player. The player who loses the ground ball plays defense, attempting to strip the ball carrier before he can make the pass.

Circle Ground Ball

Age range: beginner to experienced

Purpose: players learn to scoop balls in a crowd while protecting the stick and ball and avoiding defensive players. This prepares players for contact and teaches them to take a hit. Players also learn the skill of passing immediately after scooping.

Execution: Four lines in the shape of a diamond are formed with the players looking toward the center. The coach stands between two of the lines and a "receiver" player stands opposite him between the other two lines. The coach rolls the ball into the center of the diamond and the first player in each line (four players total) fight for the ball. The player who scoops the ground ball must keep it away from the remaining three players and pass it to the "receiver" player. Tip: use a player who needs work on his passing and catching as the receiver player. As this drill involves contact, any penalties during the exercise must be immediately called and corrected and the penalized player required to run laps or do push-ups.

Two-Man Ground Ball War

Age range: beginner to experienced

Purpose: one-on-one battle for a ground ball, using the players' leg strength and center of gravity.

Execution: players pair up and stand back-to-back with the ball between their feet. When the whistle blows, players push back using their legs until one player is able to pick up the ground ball.

Down the Line Stick Check

Age range: beginner

Purpose: teaches lateral footwork while poke checking.

Execution: players line up shoulder to shoulder on a sideline, holding their sticks out in front of them. The player at one end of the line pops out and after getting into a breakdown stance, begins a lateral shuffling down the length of the line, poke checking the sticks of his teammates as he passes. When he reaches the end, the player rejoins the line.

Ball Handling/Defense Exercise

Age range: beginner to experienced

Purpose: players with the ball work on one-handed cradling and turning away from pressure while defensive players practice footwork and drop-stepping.

Execution: lines are formed on the sideline, with an even number of players in each line and a mix of positions. The two players at the beginning of the line step forward, the player with the ball becoming the offensive player and the other taking the role of defense. The player with the ball zigzags forward at half speed toward the opposite sideline using a one-handed cradle and protecting the stick with his body and free arm. The defensive player plays mock defense, shuffling his feet and drop-stepping with the advancing offensive player, maintaining good defensive body position and forcing the offensive player to move toward open space, changing hands and directions. After all the players in the line have gone, the drill resumes from the opposite sideline with the players switching their roles of offense and defense.

Nail in the Foot

Age range: beginner

Purpose: ball protection using a one-handed cradle.

Execution: players pair up with each couple getting one ball. On the whistle, the player with the ball must maintain possession of that ball using a one-handed cradle against the attacking defender for thirty seconds. The rule is that the player with the ball cannot lift his one pivot foot while trying to avoid the defender. The pivot foot can change if the offensive player switches stick hands, but one foot must be nailed to the floor at all times. The defender cannot wrap check or encroach on the personal space of the offensive player. The defender can only use footwork and shuffling his feet to get a proper poke check on the offensive player's stick. The roles are reversed after thirty seconds have elapsed.

Conditioning Drills

Ladder Sprints

This conditioning drill emphasizes sprinting and cutting skills. Players start by lining up on the end line. At the whistle, they sprint to the first "rung" of the "ladder"—the goal line extended, where they touch the line and sprint back to the end line. They then turn and sprint to the second "rung"—the top of the restraining box, touch that line, and return to the end line. Finally, they sprint to the final "rung"—the midfield line. This drill can be performed with any type of distance markers, as long as the players return to the point of origin after touching each rung of the "ladder."

"Simon Says" Footwork

Age range: beginner to advanced

Purpose: conditioning-intense footwork drill, increasing reaction time.

Execution: the assembled group of players stand facing the coach, forming rows and lines with about five to seven yards between each player and the person behind, in front, or next to him. The coach then explains to the players that on the whistle, the players will get into a breakdown stance and begin running in place, staying on the balls of their feet and waiting for the coach's first instructions. The coach will then give a signal the players must react to. Pointing to the right or left means the players will sidestep-shuffle in that direction. When the coach points forward, the players will drop-step and backpedal. If the coach points to the ground, the players will immediately drop to lie flat on their bellies, quickly springing back up into their breakdown running-in-place stance. The second whistle ends the drill, upon which the players sprint past the coach.

CHAPTER 6

TEAM TACTICS AND PLAYBOOK

Lacrosse is a game of momentum, and a major element of the sport is playing *transition* and capitalizing on *unsettled situations* to shift momentum toward your team. Unsettled situations, which usually don't involve a whistle starting play, occur with all players ready and matched up against their opposing players on the offensive or defensive end of the field. Examples are the fast break, the slow break, broken clears, and successful rides, and they usually involve one team with an advantage in player numbers (*man up* or *man down*).

KEY TO PLAY DIAGRAM SYMBOLS		
	A	Attack
	M	Midfield
	D	Defense
	DM	Defensive Midfield
	G	Goaltender
	P	Player
	- - - >	Pass
	— >	Running Man
	P ▶	Man with Ball
	I	Set Pick
	▲	Opposing Player

Transition Play

In transition play (similar situations in hockey are called *power plays*), the team with the greater number of players has the obvious advantage. With extra attackers they can dominate the field and control the tempo, and the defense has to work harder and smarter to offset their "man down" player deficit.

Transition Formations

Example A: 2–on–1 Situation

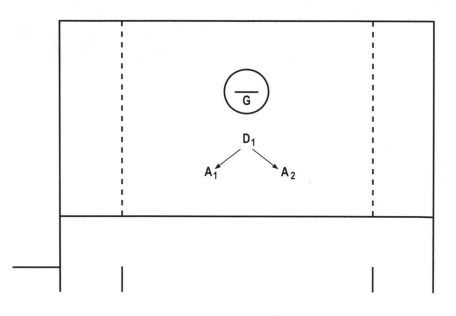

Offensive Strategy

○ **Time is against you**—The longer an offensive team waits to make a move on the goal, the more time the defense has to regroup and settle the play. If there is an opportunity to attack, take it. The second attacker, the one who does not have the ball, should think first about receiving a feed, and if it isn't coming, think next about backing up the goal.

○ **Draw and dump**—By making a purposeful, committed move toward the goal, the attacker will draw a defender out of position, allowing a pass (*dump*) to the other attackman and freeing up space for him to shoot. Without a strong move by offense, the defender can maintain his position, buying time.

O **Finish the shot**—The 2-on-1 situation should be a slam dunk. Don't waste an opportunity with a fancy trick shot or by shooting it into the goalie's chest. Throw a fake, but if you fake high, don't shoot there—fake high and shoot low. At this distance, finesse shot-placement is more important than a high-speed crank shot.

Defensive Strategy

O **No win situation**—As soon as you commit to an attacker, the attackman will typically make a pass to the open man. You have to go for the man with the ball, but you can hope to get lucky and force a bad pass or wrong move.

O **Buy time**—It is most important in this situation to buy time. This allows another defender to come back and help, or take one man, and allows the goaltender to come out of the crease to check or intercept the other attacker.

PLAYING TRANSITION DEFENSE

- Limit offensive opportunities to even the odds.

- Force outside shots that your goaltender has a better chance of stopping.

- Start playing defense inside the crease area and work your way outside. The crease position is the most dangerous and needs to be taken out of the offense's equation.

- Find the offense's weak points and exploit them. Make their feeder players take the shots, turning their best shooters into passers and limiting their shooting opportunities.

- Have defenders fall into the crease area or hole and identify (mark up) players needing to be covered. Defenders trailing the play should hustle to the hole to even the numbers. By reporting to the crease area, a defender places himself in the center of the offense, positioned to pick up any open man remaining.

- All defenders need to be on the same page and understand that they are operating as a unit.

○ **Get in close, giving up outside shots**—Position yourself in the center of the crease, careful not to screen the vision of the goaltender. Patience is important—the defender must choose the right opportunity to commit to an attacking player. If the defender rushes in early, he can cut down some of the shot angle and possibly panic the attacker, forcing him to make a bad pass or poor shot. Going later also forces a shot, but at a closer distance when a feed to another attacker is difficult. Check against your man's arms and hands, trying to lift the shooter's crosse at his moment of release.

○ **Get in a lane**—If a defender decides to wait, being in the center of the crease places him in the passing lane, and he now has the opportunity to pick off a pass or knock down the ball.

○ **Recognize players**—The player with the ball is the most dangerous, but if you must decide between committing to an average (role) player or the team's top scorer, the decision is more complicated. A goaltender may have a better opportunity to stop a role player's shot, so a defender may want to commit earlier to a top scorer.

Example B: 3–on–2 Situation

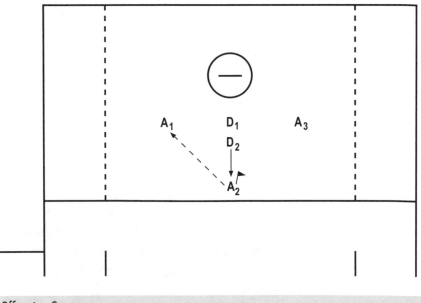

Offensive Strategy

○ **Triangle formation**—Three attackers in good shooting position form a triangle, sticks to the outside of the defense.

- ○ **Move the ball**—Moving the ball quickly and unselfishly will move the defenders. If you have the time, don't settle for an outside shot when a little work will throw off the defense and potentially free up an attacker inside.

- ○ **Draw the defender**—When you attack the goal, a defender will slide to stop you. The adjacent pass will probably be covered, so look to the weak side of the goal for an open teammate. The open player in this situation should be moving his feet, not stationary, angling for a better shot or moving away from the goal so that the goalie does not become another defender.

Defensive Strategy

- ○ **Set up an I formation**—The I formation combats the offensive triangle formation. The *high* defender (farthest from the crease) stops the ball carrier, forcing a pass. The *low* defender (closer to the crease) slides out to the wing attacker who received the ball. The high defender slides behind him (maintaining the I) to center crease, ready to move up or out to pick up the high attacker or the attacker on the opposite wing.

- ○ **Fifteen yards out**—In the I formation, stay close together and try to stop the ball at least fifteen yards from the crease. This gives the goalie a better chance at stopping a shot, and keeps defenders close enough to the attackers to make their slides.

- ○ **Stay in passing lanes**—Look for the knockdown pass, but don't chase balls. Too many defenders assume they can intercept a pass, and when they don't, they lose their defensive position or are backdoored by the attacker.

- ○ **Exercise force**—When you are down a man, going for the takeaway check is not as important as containing the attacker or forcing a bad shot. Try to force shots down and to the outside. Physically force attackers down the crease, making them choose between a crease violation, running through you, or pulling back.

- ○ **Work the gloves**—As an attacker tries to pass or shoot, get a stick on his gloves or try to lift his bottom arm, but avoid *window washing*—instinctively following the movements of your attacker's stick with your own as you try to block the shot. Instead, check on body parts that make better targets, like the arms and hands.

Example C: 4–on–3 "Fast Break" Situation

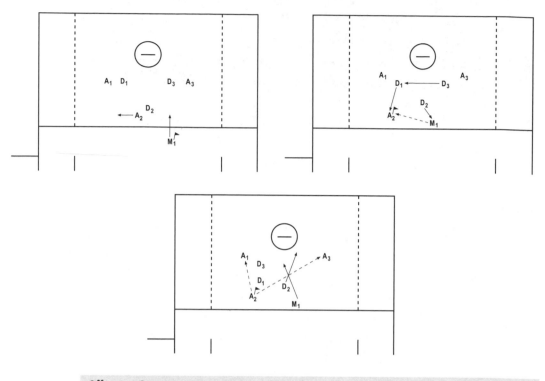

Offensive Strategy

○ **Attack triangle**—The attackmen set up their own triangle, which they can adjust to match up with the defense. A tight defensive triangle gives the attack the ability to pinch in and get a closer shot opportunity. If the defense is spaced out, the attack can then use ball movement to its advantage. A pass will move faster than a defender, and if a defender is fifteen yards from their next slide, he is already beaten.

○ **Man with ball quarterbacks**—The player who starts the fast break and carries the ball downfield decides how to execute the play. His first option is to go straight at the net. If no one stops him from streaking through the crease, he should take a solid, running bounce shot and make the defense regret its indecision. Usually, the point defenseman will pick up and slide to this breaking player. Depending on which side of the field the point attackman is set up, the player carrying the ball should come down on the opposite side.

- **Move ball opposite**—Once the point defender is forced to slide, attack the direction the slide came from. By passing the ball opposite to the point attackman, the defense will find itself trying to catch up.

- **Skip pass**—Defenders fall into a pattern during fast breaks, anticipating the pass and sliding early, hoping the passing attackman doesn't notice and is just going through the motions. This is the perfect opportunity for a *skip pass* (that is, a pass that "skips" the order of rotation). If the defender leaves his man early, the point attackman can pass directly to his teammate. This man will be positioned diagonally opposite him and is often open and able to shoot point-blank at the goal.

Defensive Strategy

- **Keep a tight triangle**—Set up a tight triangle, with defenders about ten yards apart. One defender plays the point, with two defenders left and right on the crease. The point defender stops the ball when the attacker gets within fifteen yards of the cage. A tight triangle positions players close enough to make their slides.

- **Point man slide**—The point defender is the key to defensive rotation and must let his teammates know that he is point and is ready for the break. The point man should not commit to a slide until the offense is within shooting distance, disregarding earlier passes and maneuvering among the attackers. Many defenders get into the habit of sliding as soon as the initial ball carrier passes, even when the play is still a distance from the cage. The point defender positions himself an even distance between the initial ball carrier and the point attackman and waits until one gets within shooting range before sliding. Be patient, they could make two or three passes before one of them is a threat within your designated triangle.

- **Always rotate**—Rotation direction is determined by the initial slide and moves in the opposite direction of the offensive pass. If a midfielder on a fast break comes down the left side of the field and the point man slides to him, the right defender will slide upfield in a counterclockwise motion.

○ **Slide option**—You can delay a slide, but someone must always move to stop the ball. The point defender typically goes for the ball carrier, but when it is carried by a less dangerous player, like a long pole, he can choose to lock onto the point attackman and force the long-pole player to keep the ball, denying him a pass opportunity. One of the lower defensemen then slides to stop this ball carrier when he gets within shooting distance.

○ **Open up**—The point defender, after his initial slide, is responsible for sliding to an attackman closer to the crease (that player will depend on the slide rotation). The defender needs to slide with his stick out in front, watching the offense's skip pass lane to prevent a pass.

Example D: 4–on–3 "Flat Break" Situation for advanced players

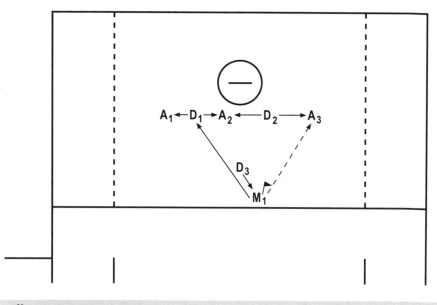

Offensive Strategy

○ **No point attackman**—In the flat break, the point attackman sinks into the crease area, positioning himself behind the point defender, in front of the cage, between the two wing attackmen.

○ **Confused defense**—When the point attackman sinks low, his defender must decide to go with him or maintain the defensive triangle. If the defender follows, he leaves no other defender to act as the point, and the man carrying the ball has a lane to the cage. If the point defender stays in his triangle, the attackman who sank low needs to make himself a threat on the crease, pulling one of the wing defenders in to help, allowing a wing at-tackman to pinch in as well, which gets the attackman in position for a pass and a great shot opportunity.

Defensive Strategy

○ **Maintain the triangle**—As in the fast break, the defense should stay in its triangle, stopping the ball farther from the crease.

○ **Pinch and react**—By sharing responsibilities, two low defense-men can cover three attackmen when necessary, moving back and forth between the attackers in reaction to wherever the ball is passed.

○ **Don't forget the goalie**—Your goaltender has some defensive ability as well. An attackman standing on the crease runs the risk of a charging goaltender leveling him if he allows himself to get too close.

Example E: 5-on-4 Situation

Offensive Strategy

○ **More options**—In this formation, the offense has the option to add a man behind the goal (a position generally referred to as X) or to bring that player into the crease.

○ With a man at X, the offense has a "quarterback" who can visu-alize the field, make feeds, or attack the cage directly from behind.

○ Another option is to position a crease man. This adds another player to the mix, forcing four defenders to cover five men in front of the cage.

Defensive Strategy

○ **Box it up**—The defense places itself in a box formation, rotating in the shape of a square. The point defender directs the defensive midfielder. Sticks should be pointed inside the lane, which is a deterrent to passing and helps cover the crease attackmen or knock down passes.

○ **COMA slide**—The COMA slide is field language for "coming across the crease." In situations when an X attackman circles around to the front of the cage, the closest defender prevents the draw and dump by shutting off the adjacent pass, while the far crease defender slides across the crease (in front of the goalie) to pick up the man with the ball. This leaves the attackman open on the other side of the goal, but places a defender and the goalie between him and the passer.

Rides and Clears

A *settled clear* is when a team moves the ball upfield after a whistle starts play. The clearing team not only has the ball, it has an extra man (its goalie) to help, and therefore the numbers advantage. At some point, the team's opponents will need to cover two men with one player or resort to zone play. The short-pole midfielders will be most heavily covered (by the opposing or *riding* team), and they have to try to get open, using V-cuts and curling back while being careful not to bring defenders toward their teammates with the ball. Whenever possible, the ball should be passed to open short-stick players, who are better able to move the ball upfield in the offensive area. It's also a good idea to advance the ball on the side of the field opposite the substitution box—this area has too much activity with players entering and leaving the field.

The *settled ride* combats the settled clear, giving the team not in possession of the ball time to place its players into position, which is critical because they are outnumbered. The riding team in the opponent's defensive area could force a turnover leading to an easy score because the goalie is out of the crease and advancing upfield with the ball carriers. Midfielders on the riding team must play tight on the players they are guarding to deny their opponents an easy pass at center field. In man-to-man coverage, riding players also must follow their opponents, even if they cross the midfield line, to prevent an offside call. Meanwhile, the riding attackmen set up a zone above the crease (the *high crease* area) and must be ready to slide to cover the defensemen and goalie advancing the ball.

A riding team should work to delay the clear by turning the clearing players back or forcing a bad pass that goes out of bounds or is intercepted. A strong physical defense, with lots of contact and hard body checking, is more effective here than stick checking, which often as not results in an opponent breaking free to find an opening for a pass or shot. Although rides have limited success in defeating a clear, they are not without opportunities—a riding team playing hard can force a turnover or even make its opponents exceed the allotted ten-second possession time in that area of the field.

Offensive Formations

In lacrosse, offensive formations (also referred to as *sets*) are described using numbers that indicate the positions of the offensive players in relation to the goal. For example, a 1–3–2 set means one man is behind the crease, three men are just in front of the crease, and two men are at the top of the box.

Offensive players should keep themselves well spread out. A tightly grouped offense makes playing defense an easier task. Coaches typically teach their players to use as much of the field as necessary and to use the restraining lines as a guide to gauge their position. Because lacrosse is a running sport, players find themselves upfield one minute and downfield the next. Movement is part of the game, but each player must maintain his focus and be constantly aware of the offensive set he is in at any given time. When players rotate and replace in formations, maintaining the integrity of the formation is key.

The position or man behind the crease is known as X. The X position in offense is important for a number of reasons. First, by moving the ball behind the goal, it helps to slow the tempo of the game and gives the offense time to settle down and settle into formation. Not many defenders will chase a ball to X aggressively because that player is not a direct threat to score. Once X has the ball, however, this becomes a dangerous feeding position. The X player can see the entire field and offense in front of him. When the defense leaves a player behind the cage, unguarded with the ball, it is an invitation for an assist. Finally, the X position is vital for retaining possession after shots. If a ball goes out of bounds on a shot, the player closest to it when it crosses the line (any player, offensive or defensive) is awarded possession. The X player is also near the end line, and if you don't have an attackman there on a shot, the goaltender usually beats everyone else to win possession. If your team has the green light to shoot, make sure someone has filled the X spot.

Example A: 1–3–2

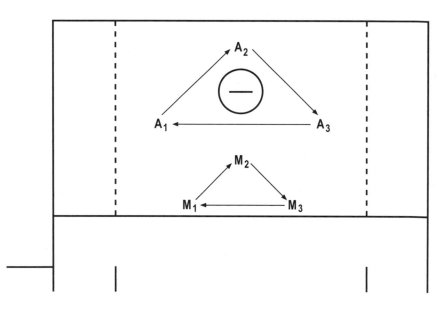

This is the most basic formation in lacrosse. The 1–3–2 is designed like two stacked triangles, one attack and one midfield. Players should rotate and make replacements within their respective triangles, maintaining the integrity of the formations.

One attackman positions himself behind the goal, at the X position. This player acts as a feeder and, more important, backs up the goal on shots.

Two attackmen position themselves on the wings, just above the goal line extended, ready to shoot or draw a defender and dump the ball to a teammate, preferably the crease man.

One midfielder is on the crease, screening the goalie's vision and looking to get open for the point-blank shot. When the ball moves behind goal to X, the crease man should move higher in the crease, closer to the restraining line. When the ball is with the topside midfielders or the wing attack, this crease man should position himself lower in the crease.

Two midfielders are at the top of the box, ready to fall back onto defense or take outside shots. These players should be expecting picks from the crease man so they can cut to the cage. The middies may also choose to isolate or "iso" their defender and attempt to beat him one-on-one. In this case, their teammates must clear out for them, moving across the field to draw away any defensive slides or help.

Example B: 1–4–1 for advanced players

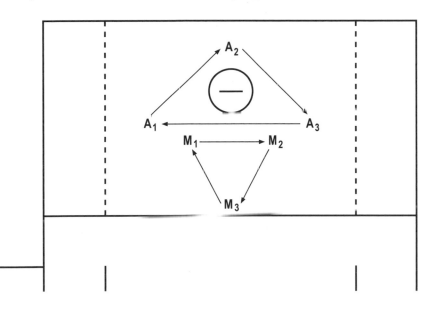

The 1–4–1 keeps one player at X, but reduces the midfield to one player near the restraining line. Four players are spread across the field just above the goal line extended, with two players in the crease position.

The topside midfielder is entirely responsible for preventing the fast break if a turnover occurs. The midfielder now also acts as a feeder to the attack on the wings, similar to the X position. As noted earlier, this midfielder should avoid forcing feeds to the crease, as those players will have their backs to the goal and can't easily shoot.

The addition of a crease player to the formation is one of the great benefits of the 1–4–1. Two crease men can set picks for one another, confuse defensive slides, and are very effective in screening the goalie's vision. Wing attackmen are looking for feeds to the crease, or can pinch toward the goal when they get an opportunity to shoot.

Example C: 2–2–2 for advanced players

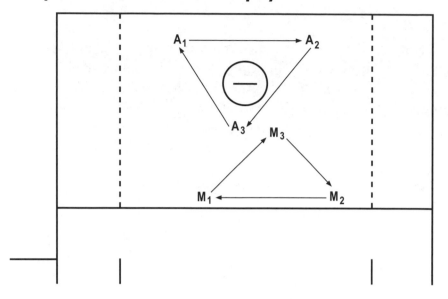

The 2–2–2 is a stacked offense, with two players behind the goal, two crease men, and two players at the top of the restraining box.

Again, there is the benefit of two crease men, but these crease players position themselves high. The two attackmen behind the cage will push the ball to the goal, drawing the defense low, allowing the crease players to backdoor their defenders and cut to the net.

The two midfielders at the top of the restraining box also need to remain high, as the crease men will be playing a high crease. These four players will rotate, attempting to draw a short-stick defender onto an attackman.

Defensive Fundamentals

When playing defense, it is sometimes smart to think offensively. Don't simply react to what the offense brings—dictate what you want the offense to do. Changing game tempo and varying defensive schemes are a good way to throw off an offense and maintain field superiority.

BASIC RULES OF DEFENSE

- Rule number one: contain your man.

- Defense is played with your feet, not with your stick.

- Dictate to the offense where you want it to go.

- Force your man to an area you choose—push offense to outside, downside of goal.

- Make it difficult for attackmen to get upfield.

- Anticipate offensive strategy—think two passes ahead.

- Meet all opponents with a poke check.

- Man watch, don't ball watch—let the goalie keep track of the ball and relay information to the defense.

- Never allow a ball to be received where opponent can immediately score or assist.

- Take away receptions by sliding as the ball is thrown, not after the ball is received.

- Take away X, especially if that man runs the show.

- Check every pass and every catch.

- Shut off potent offensive players with short-stick defensive midfielders.

- When you slide to the ball carrier, slide to where he will be, not where he is.

- Remember to "think like a BUM" (Ball-U-Man)—always position "U" (you) between the Ball and the Man you are guarding.

Slides

The *slide* is a key defensive movement in lacrosse. Basically, it's when defenders shift position in reaction to specific situations—such as when a ball-carrying opponent breaks free of (*beats*) the man covering him, or

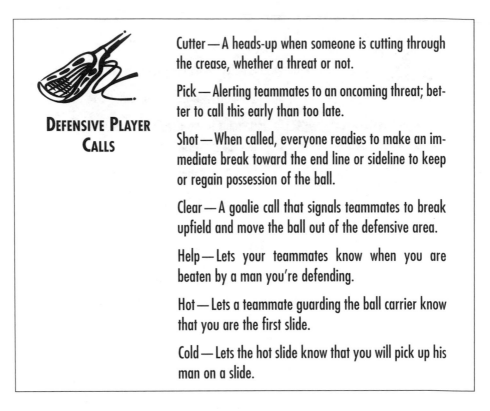

DEFENSIVE PLAYER CALLS

Cutter — A heads-up when someone is cutting through the crease, whether a threat or not.

Pick — Alerting teammates to an oncoming threat; better to call this early than too late.

Shot — When called, everyone readies to make an immediate break toward the end line or sideline to keep or regain possession of the ball.

Clear — A goalie call that signals teammates to break upfield and move the ball out of the defensive area.

Help — Lets your teammates know when you are beaten by a man you're defending.

Hot — Lets a teammate guarding the ball carrier know that you are the first slide.

Cold — Lets the hot slide know that you will pick up his man on a slide.

to pick up (*cover*) an open receiver moving into scoring position. Deciding who among the defending players slides to which opponent depends on the situation and formation.

Slides have a cascading effect, and are typically carried out in two movements: in the initial *hot* slide, one man moves to cover an opponent, usually to stop the ball; in the second *cold* slide, a teammate moves into his position and this begins a rotation where the remaining defenders move to fill other positions. The hot slide is crucial to stopping the ball, but the cold slide is nearly as important. When the defense slides from man to man, the offense usually attempts to move the ball in the opposite direction, looking for an open receiver.

In lacrosse, there are two basic defense formations—*man-to-man* (each man defending an individual player), and *zone* (each man covering a specific area or zone of the field). Within man-to-man defense, there are two types of slides: the *adjacent slide* and the *crease slide*. Adjacent slides originate with defenders on the left or right (adjacent to) of the defender covering the man with the ball. Crease slides originate only with a defender who is covering an offensive player positioned in the crease.

Adjacent Slide

In the adjacent slide defense, two designated defenders have responsibility for initiating the slide if the defender covering the ball is beaten by the offense. These *hot slide* players are known as *help left* and *help right*. If the ball defender is beaten to the right, the slide comes from the right, and vice versa. In guarding their own men, the slide defenders must hang back slightly (*sag*) toward the crease, anticipating the slide, so they will be positioned in front of the ball carrier when needed.

Because adjacent slides counter-rotate to the offensive flow, if the hot slide comes from the right, the cold slide will be the teammate from his right, and so on. In keeping with this circular rotation, when an attackman rolls toward the goal from behind the crease, the defenseman on the far side of the goal makes the cross-crease hot slide (COMA slide). The crease defender in this formation never slides—he stays locked onto the man he is covering.

The adjacent slide makes for a good basic defense package. It is easily learned and run, especially by a novice team, and passes are kept out of the crease by the locked-on defender. There are flaws to this defense as well. Because the defense sags back, taking pressure off the adjacent offensemen, it makes it easier for the ball carrier to pass to his teammates, which gives the offense time to find an opportunity to score.

Example A: Adjacent Slides

Man-to-Man versus 2–2–2 Offense for advanced players

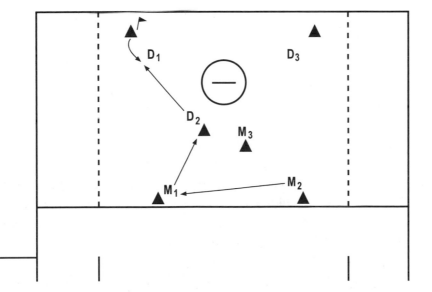

D1 (Defender 1) is beat on a dodge to his left, so D2 becomes the hot slide with M1 (Midfielder 1) as the cold slide. M3 stays locked on his man, M2 slides to the man vacated by M1.

Man-to-Man versus 1–3–2 Offense for advanced players

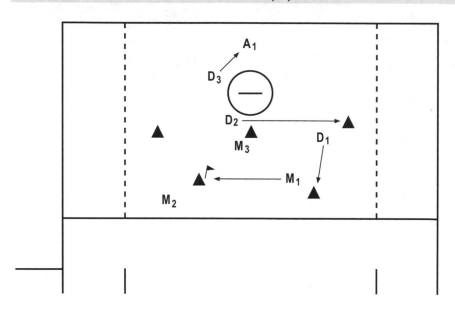

M2 is beat to his left, making M1 the hot slide and D1 the cold slide. M3 stays locked on his crease offenseman. D2 slides to the man vacated by D1. D3 covers X and M2 slides to cover the man vacated by D2.

Crease Slide

In this defense, the hot slide comes only from the crease. The defender covering the offensive crease player must always be ready for the slide, positioning his body between the ball and the man he is covering. Hot and cold crease slides move in a straight line (*on the string*) with the ball carrier at one end, the hot slide in the middle, and the cold slide at the far end. The cold slide is the key to this defense. The player he covers is almost always farthest from the ball. This allows the cold slide to help cover the hot slide's man, which lets the hot slide move closer to the ball carrier. This support allows the hot slide to go early and with conviction, double-teaming the ball carrier or moving into slide position before it is needed.

The defenders adjacent to the ball carrier have no slide responsibility, allowing them to keep heavy pressure on their offensive opponents. A rule of thumb in crease slides is "One pass away, one step away." That is, if your man is the first pass from the ball carrier, your defensive position should be one step away from that player. If your man is two or more passes from the ball carrier, you are eligible to assist the crease slide defender. By shutting off the adjacent pass, a defender forces the heavily pressured offense to make skip passes or very difficult cross-field passes.

Crease slides are a very aggressive defense. The hot slide player is positioned to move when needed, or can double up on the ball carrier. Because only the crease defender initiates the slide, there is no confusion about who goes to the ball. Drawbacks include the fact that the cold slide's man will always be open—if that man makes a move, the cold slide must drop back to cover, leaving the hot slide without backup. Also, because the slide comes from the crease, the defense faces the threat of leaving a dangerous offensive player wide open in front of its goal.

Example B: Crease Slides

Man-to-Man versus 2–2–2 Offense for advanced players

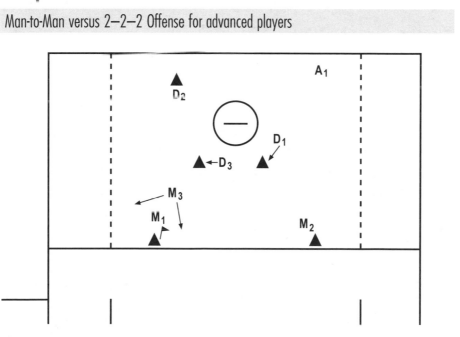

Against the 2–2–2, the offense employs two crease players, so the defense must determine which of the two defenders covering the crease will be the hot slide. In this example, M3 is the first slide. D1 falls back to the hole to help D3 with the two crease players. D1 and D3 maintain a crease zone, each playing a side, so one isn't drawn too far away from

X, which would allow that attackman to circle the crease. Here, A1 (Attackman 1) is deliberately left open to allow D1 to help in the crease. M2 and D2 put heavy adjacent pressure on their opponents. If the two crease men overload the left side, M3 must fall back from his slide to help.

Man-to-Man versus 1–4–1 Offense for advanced players

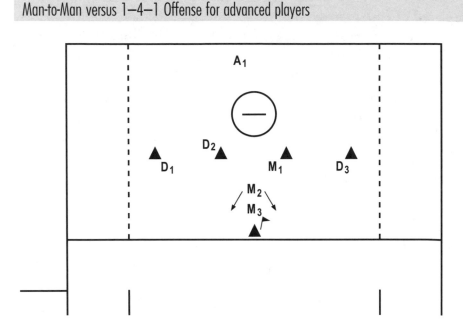

If M3 is beaten, M2 is the hot slide. D2, who was guarding A1 (A1 is the X attackman and farthest from the ball), becomes the cold slide and leaves to help in the crease. D1 and D3 pressure their opponents to guard against an adjacent pass. Now the ball carrier's only passing option is through the crease to X, and through five defensive sticks.

Playing the Zone

The other type of lacrosse defense formation is the zone defense. Unlike the man-to-man defense with players covering individual opponents, here players are responsible for specific positions on the field, primarily around the goal.

The example shown places four long-pole defenders in a box formation—one man on each goal post and two men forward of the goal (see diagram on next page). This creates a defensive perimeter manned by four players armed with formidable weaponry. Within this zone, two short-stick midfielders are "stacked" in front of the crease, positioned to deny passes from the outside and take on attackers threatening the goal.

Zones are useful as an alternative to man-to-man defenses and when playing in a "man down" situation. In a zone, the men stationed around and in front of the goal prevent passes into the crease, create a barrier to deter charging attackers, and force opponents to take more low-percentage outside shots. Zones also work well against designed plays because the zone players are not covering individuals and are less susceptible to picks. A few strong players can even shut down an opposing team. But if a lacrosse team uses a zone defense, it usually does not rely on it for long. Although zones can confuse an offense for a time, opponents soon enough find the holes in the defense, and the benefits of a zone become liabilities. Without constant pressure from the defense, the offense controls the ball and can take more of those outside shots, bombarding the goaltender. The zone is also a rigid defense, handcuffing a team's best defenders and limiting their ability to play an aggressive one-on-one game.

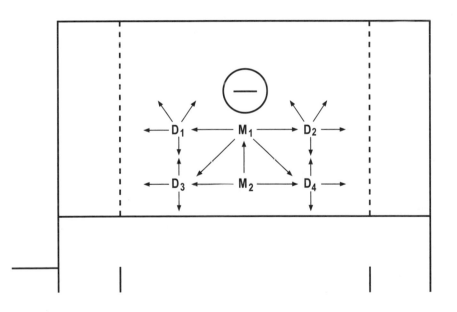

Basic Zone (Box) Defense

Defenders D1 and D2 are stationed at the goal posts, covering the area right and left of the goal, directly in front and just above the crease. Long-poles D3 and D4 are the wing defenders, guarding outside almost to the restraining line. Midfielder M1 covers low in the crease, and is responsible for the area directly in front of the goal. M2 plays higher in the crease and areas between D3 and D4.

Specialty Formation

Defense Lock-Off (Blackjack)

Blackjack is a defensive lock-off on all players that isolates everyone away from the man with the ball. This play shouldn't be used against an opposing team's star offensive player, but it is very effective when a dominant defender is matched up against a weaker ball handler. The idea is to trap the player with the ball in a no-outlet situation, allowing the defender to attempt a takeaway (steal). The offensive player either submits to the stronger defender or throws the ball away. Assign your best takeaway man to the job, preferably someone who isn't prone to penalties. All other offensive players on the field must be locked off—regardless of where they run or dodge on the field, their defenders stay jersey to jersey with them, preventing them from getting open at any time to receive a pass. There is no slide in this play, so a defender can't allow himself to get beat.

Offensive Plays

There are any number of plays a team can invent, improvise, borrow, or even steal from other teams. Often, teams give their plays code names (the Bruins, for example, may dub their plays Grizzly, Kodiak, etc.) or use words that make some mental association (Syracuse for a sweep, Purdue for a pick, etc.). Here are six classic offensive plays—call them whatever you want—that may be used as is or with variations your team might want to add.

Pass and Pick Away

This is a basic pass-and-pick-away situation out of the 1–3–2 formation, ending in a point-blank shot by a midfielder in front of the crease:

1. M3 has possession and passes the ball to M1.
2. Immediately after passing the ball, M3 sets a pick for M2.
3. M2 circles off the pick and receives a pass from M1, which gives M2 protection for a shot on goal.

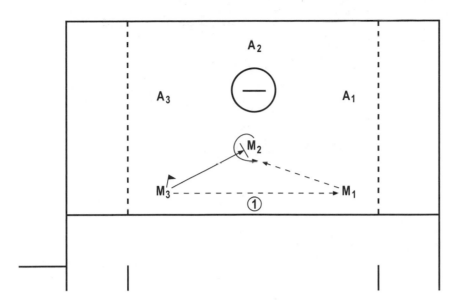

Double Pick

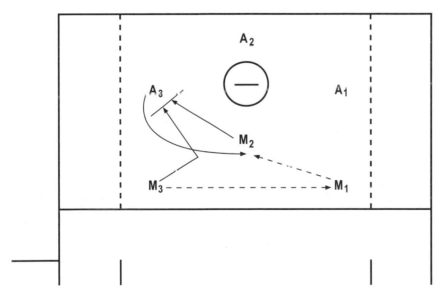

This play, which builds from the Pass and Pick Away play, fools the defense into believing the same play is coming out of the 1–3–2 formation. Instead the offense adds a double-player pick and moves the ball to the attackmen, who take the shot.

1. M3 passes to M1.

2. M3 cuts toward M2 as though he is setting a pick for him, but

then veers off. Now shoulder to shoulder with M2, the two set a pick for A3.

3.   A3 comes off the double pick and M1 passes the ball to him.

4.   If A3 is not open, M3 and M2 can roll off the pick and follow A3, all of them looking for a pass.

Midfield Sweep for advanced players

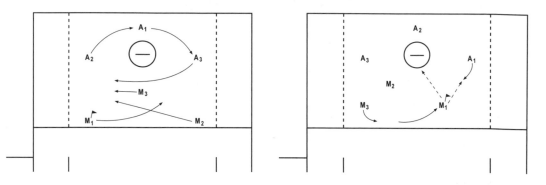

In this sweep play, the other offensive players in the 1–3–2 formation clear out of the way, allowing a midfielder to isolate his defender in a one-on-one situation and then run across the field to take a moving shot.

1.   M1 starts with the ball and calls the play.

2.   The midfield and attack begin a triangular rotation: M2 cuts all the way through the crease. At the same time, A3 makes a similar crease-cutting motion to replace for A2, who moves up to fill the X position. A1 rotates to where A3 originated.

Second Movement

3.   As the offense settles into position, M1 begins his one-on-one challenge with his defender, "sweeping" across the field and taking a running shot at the best angle he can gain.

4.   If no shot is available, M1 can pass to A1, who has moved into shooting position.

Quick Shot 1–4–1 for advanced players

A perfect play out of the 1–4–1 formation for a last-ditch shot, this is only good for one attempt, but it is excellent for catching the opposing team off guard and scoring a goal in the final seconds to tie a game.

1.   Position your best shooting attackman in the A2 position.

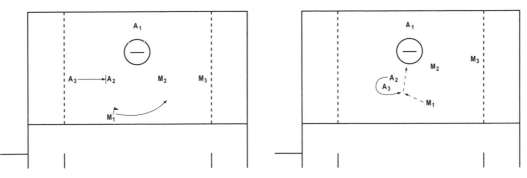

2. Start the ball with M1, who makes it look as though he is sweeping toward the goal for a right-handed shot.

3. When M1 begins his fake sweep, A3 breaks in from the wing and sets a pick for A2.

Second Movement

4. A2 curls off the pick and receives a cross-body pass from the sweeping M1.

5. A2 takes a quick shot while M2 screens the goalie (M2 must be careful not to place himself in the line of the shot).

Stack Play

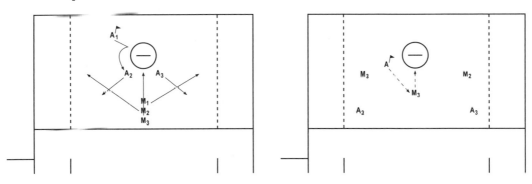

A simple midfield stack play that can be run after a whistle resumes play from behind the cage, resulting in a midfielder shot.

1. A1 begins with the ball on the end line, while A2 and A3 screen the goalie in a double-crease position.

2. M1, M2, and M3 line up in a vertical stack with M1 closest to the goal. These players maintain a distance of two feet between them, and should be just inside the restraining box.

3. After players have taken their positions, A1 will a drive the

cage, feigning that he is the shooter.

4. When A1 begins his drive, A2 and A3 break upfield and out, clearing the crease area.

5. M1 breaks downfield toward the right wing, and M2 breaks downfield toward the left wing, drawing their men while signaling for the ball.

6. M3, the intended shooter, breaks straight toward the cage, his path clear since A1, A2, M1, and M2 have drawn their men out of the crease and toward the outside wings.

7. A1 passes to M3 for the shot.

Sideline Play

Another stack play, this time resulting in an attackman's shot. This play can be run off the whistle when a ball is returned to play after going out of bounds.

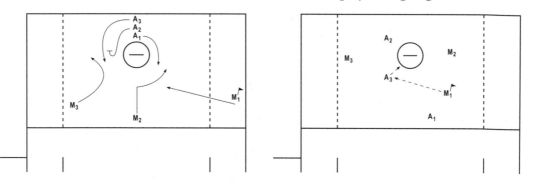

1. M1 starts with the ball on the sideline, on either side of the field.

2. A1, A2, and A3 form a vertical stack behind the cage, with A3 closest to the end line. A3 will be your shooter.

3. M2 and M3 position themselves high in the restraining box, M2 taking the center of the field and M3 standing opposite field side from M1.

4. When M1 begins to bring the ball in bounds, A1 breaks around the crease toward M1 and cuts upfield. M2 and M3 begin cutting toward the cage as decoys, calling for the ball from M1.

5. Just after A1 begins his cut, A2 breaks around the crease in the direction opposite A1, feigning the same movement. Instead A2 stops short of goal line extended and turns, setting a pick for A3 who comes around the cage for the shot.

6. M1 feeds A3 for the shot.

CHAPTER 7

INFORMATION AND RESOURCES

Leagues

Collegiate Level Lacrosse

Division I Conferences:
ACC—Atlantic Coast Conference
America East
Colonial
ECAC—Eastern College Athletic Conference
Great Western
Ivy League
MAAC—Metro Atlantic Athletic Conference
Patriot League

Division II Conferences:
Deep South
New York Collegiate Athletic Conference
Northeast-10
Independents

Division III Conferences:
Capital Athletic
Centennial

Commonwealth Coast
Empire 8
Knickerbocker
Little East
Middle Atlantic
NESCAC—New England Small College Athletic Conference
North Coast
Old Dominion
Pennsylvania
Pilgrim League
SUNYAC—State University of New York Athletic Conference
UCAA—Upstate Collegiate Athletic Association (Liberty League)
Independents

Junior College League

No conferences (twenty-six schools)

Intercollegiate Associates

Conferences:
CCLA—Central Collegiate Lacrosse Association
GRLC—Great Rivers Lacrosse Conference
LSA—Lone Star Alliance
PNCLL—Pacific Northwest Collegiate Lacrosse League
PCLL—Pioneer Collegiate Lacrosse League
RMILL—Rocky Mountain Intercollegiate Lacrosse League
SELC—Southeastern Lacrosse Conference
UMLL—Upper Midwest Lacrosse League
WCLL—Western Collegiate Lacrosse League

Postcollegiate Club Lacrosse

American Lacrosse League
Blue Conference (New England, New Jersey, New York,
   Pennsylvania Divisions)
Grey Conference (East, South, West Divisions)
Desert Lacrosse League
Florida Lacrosse League
Great Plains Lacrosse League
Gulf Coast Lacrosse League

Midwest Cities Lacrosse League
Northern California Lacrosse Association
Southeast Lacrosse League
    East Division
    West Division
Southwest Lacrosse Association
United States Club Lacrosse Association
    Empire Division
    Northern Division
    Southern Division
Yankee League

Major League Lacrosse

Eastern Division

Baltimore Bayhawks
New Jersey Pride
Rochester Rattlers

American Division

Boston Cannons
Long Island Lizards
Philadelphia Barrage

Western Division

(to debut 2006)
Los Angeles
San Francisco
Denver
Chicago

Lacrosse Equipment

Manufacturers

Brine, Inc.
47 Sumner Street
Milford, MA 01757
www.brine.com

STX, Inc.
1500 Bush Street
Baltimore, MD 21230
1–800–368–2250
www.stxlacrosse.com

Warrior Lacrosse, Inc.
6881 Chicago Street
Warren, MI 48092
1–800–968–7845
www.warriorlacrosse.com

deBeer Lacrosse
P.O. Box 11–570
Albany, NY 12211
www.debeerlacrosse.com

Shamrock Lacrosse
635 Ramsey Avenue, #102B
Hillside, NJ 07205
1–800–308–4529
www.shamrocklax.com

Harrow Sports, Inc.
Denver, CO
1–800–541–2905
www.harrowsports.com

Stryke Lacrosse
24100 Gibson Street
Warren, MI 48089
1–866–STRYKE1
www.strykelacrosse.com

Gait Helmets, LLC
318 S. Clinton Street
Syracuse, NY 13202
1–800–530–0280
www.gaithelmets.com

National Equipment Retailers

Bacharach Rasin
802 Gleneagles Court
Towson, MD 21286
1–800–726–2468
www.bacharach.com

Lax World
Kenilworth Park Mall
Towson, MD 21204
1–410–321–7333
www.laxworld.com

Commonwealth Lacrosse
400 Washington Street
Weymouth, MA 02188
1–888–LIV–4LAX (548–4529)
www.comlax.net

Great Atlantic Lacrosse Company
Old Wyler's Dock
P.O. Box 16872
Chapel Hill, NC 27516
1–800–955–3876
www.lacrosse.com

Queen City Lacrosse
200 Villani Drive
Suite 3007
Bridgeville, PA 15017
1–800–240–0178
www.qclax.com

GLOSSARY

Assist—A pass that precedes and directly contributes to a scored goal. For an assist to be awarded to the passer, the scoring player must not make any move or take any action that beats a defender other than the goalkeeper.

Attackmen—A team's three players positioned closest to the opponent's goal on the offensive side of the field. These players are typically the team's most potent scorers and generally remain in the offensive area.

Ball movement—Passing the ball among players while in an offensive formation.

Beat—To outmaneuver another player.

Body check—When a player deliberately collides with an opponent in an attempt to knock the ball loose, knock the player down, or stop the opponent's momentum.

Breakdown—A proper defensive stance, with feet shoulder-width apart and knees bent to lower the center of gravity.

Cage—Slang term for the lacrosse goal and net.

Check—Using the body or stick to hit another player; a legal move in an attempt to dislodge the ball.

Clear—The act of moving the ball upfield and out of the defensive area following a shot or turnover.

Conditioning—Exercises that help to increase stamina and strength.

Cradle (Cradling)—The combined movement of a player's arms, hands, and stick to create the centrifugal force necessary to keep a ball in the stick pocket.

Crease—A circle with a nine-foot radius that surrounds the lacrosse goal on each end of the field.

Crosse (Stick)—The instrument used to pass and catch in the sport of lacrosse. The stick consists of a shaft, usually made of aluminum or titanium, and a plastic head with string netting.

Defender—Any player opposing the team in possession of the ball.

Defensive midfield line—A player formation that specializes in defense or in recovering the ball from the opposing team.

Defensive specialist—A skilled player who enters the game in situations where his team is attempting to retrieve the ball from the opposing team or prevent their opponents from scoring. Long-stick midfielders are an example of defensive specialists.

Double-team—When two (or more) defenders assist in attacking or defending a single opponent.

Drill—A live exercise that teaches or practices a skill or play.

Drop step—The motion of moving one's foot one step rearward while in a breakdown stance in order to maintain proper defensive positioning against an advancing opponent.

Fast break—The rapid advance of an unguarded ball carrier into a team's defensive zone; this usually results in a greater offensive-to-defensive player ratio.

Field balance—Equal distribution of offensive players in the offensive zone as dictated by the formation being used.

Field communication—Onfield "chatter" between teammates, such as when a goalie directs the defense in a slide, or when players call and echo strategies or plays.

Footwork—A player's stance, speed, and balance, usually as it relates to proper positioning and physical presence rather than stick skills for effective defense.

Fundamentals—The basic elements of lacrosse, including rules, player skills, field movements, plays, and other information essential to a solid, well-rounded game.

Goalie (Goaltender)—A specially-equipped defensive player positioned in the crease whose primary duty is to protect the goal.

Institute of International Sport (www.internationalsport.com)—A nonprofit organization, founded in 1986, that fosters improved relations between nations by encouraging youth sports, individual growth, ethical behavior, and good sportsmanship.

Isolation or "iso"—Game situation where the ball carrier attempts to isolate a defender and outmaneuver (beat) him in order to shoot on goal.

Lacrosse—A ball sport that originated among the native tribes of North America. Called *bagataway* by these tribes, the game later became known among colonial settlers as lacrosse, a French term for cross or crutch, which described the stick used in play.

Lift—A type of defensive check where the defender uses his stick to elevate an opponent's gloves, arms, or stick in an attempt to dislodge the ball, or to prevent him from shooting or throwing.

Line drills—A practice or pregame drill in which groups of players line up facing each other and cycle through a series of warm-up exercises such as passing and catching, ground balls, and light defense.

Man-to-man defense—A strategy where each player targets a particular opponent and becomes responsible for guarding him wherever he goes on the field.

Midfielder (Middie)—A player whose position requires movement to both the offensive and defensive sides of the field, and who performs in offensive and defensive capacities as needed.

MVP—"Most Valuable Player."

National Alliance for Youth Sports (NAYS) (www.nays.org)—A leading advocate for responsible and safe youth sports. This nonprofit organization, based in Florida, provides assistance and training for coaches, educators, and other sports officials with an emphasis on instilling character and values in youth players.

Net—The string mesh enclosing the goal that traps the ball after a shot; also a slang term for the goal itself, or cage.

Off-ball movements—Actions taken by offensive players who are not carrying the ball; this includes cutting, setting picks, and rotating offensive positions.

Offside—The illegal movement of a player onto another half of the field, resulting in too few players on a side.

Pinnies—Practice jerseys, often reversible with team colors on one side and "home white" on the other for scrimmage use.

Point position—The leading attackman of an offensive triangle formation in a fast-break situation.

Poke (poke check)—A type of stick check where a spearing motion is used to dislodge the ball or disrupt an offensive player's throwing and catching.

Positive Coaching Alliance (PCA) (www.positivecoach.org)—Founded in 1998, this organization emphasizes sportsmanship over winning, and offers workshops for parents, coaches, and educators to help engage and retain youth players in sports.

Restraining box—A delineated section of the field; the term refers to the fact that players are held within this area during face-offs until possession is called.

Ride—An offensive team strategy used to prevent an opposing team from advancing the ball out of the defensive area after a shot or a turnover.

Scooping—A shoveling motion with the stick that is used to pick up a ground ball.

Scrimmage—A practice game among teammates, or a game between opposing teams that has no value in regular season standings.

Sets—A term used to describe various offensive formations available to a team.

Settled play—Any game play that isn't a fast break or loose ball situation; also, an even playing situation where both defense and offense teams are in position.

Sideline clear—The act of moving the ball out of the defensive area (from the sideline) following a whistle after a dead-ball situation; this action typically results from an out-of-bounds ball.

Slap—A type of stick check where the defensive player hits the stick or gloves of a ball carrier with a lateral (horizontal) motion.

Slide—When a defending player leaves a man or position he is covering to counter an offensive threat.

Slow break—A strategy where the ball is moved by the offense to the X position during transition play to gain time, maintain possession, and settle the players into formation. It is usually called when a *fast break* is disrupted or when the offense wants to substitute players.

Squad—A general term that refers to any group of players or an entire team.

Stick (see Crosse)

Stick length—The legal limit of a lacrosse stick. Short sticks must measure between 40 and 42 inches, and long sticks must measure between 52 and 72 inches. Goalie sticks can measure between 40 and 72 inches.

Substitution—When one player is sent onto the field to replace another.

Transition play—Any game situation that indicates a team change from offensive to defensive action, or from defense to offense.

Unsettled play—Game action referring to any unstructured play such as fast breaks or uneven numbers. Typically, unsettled play starts spontaneously, without a whistle from the referee, when teams are not in set offensive and defensive positions.

Wind sprints—Fast running exercises that promote physical conditioning.

"X"—The playing area between the back of the crease and the endline. In field language, X can also refer to an attackman playing within that area.

Zone defense—Unlike the man-to-man defense, this strategy positions players to guard specific areas of the field, with each man responsible for defending any offensive player that enters his zone.

INDEX